Come-Ons, Comebacks,
AND
Kiss-Offs

Also by Jeanne Martinet

The Art of Mingling

Getting Beyond Hello

The Faux Pas Survival Guide

Come-Ons, Comebacks,

AND

Kiss-Offs

DATE LINES EVERY   WOMAN NEEDS

TO SURVIVE   HER SEARCH

FOR THE HOLY MALE

Jeanne Martinet

ST. MARTIN'S GRIFFIN

NEW YORK

DESIGN BY JUDITH STAGNITTO ABBATE

Library of Congress Cataloging-in-Publication Data

Martinet, Jeanne
    Come-ons, comebacks, and kiss-offs : date lines every woman needs to survive her search for the holy male / Jeanne Martinet.
        p.   cm.
    ISBN 0-312-16809-8
    1. Dating (Social customs)   2. Man-woman relationships.
3. Conversation.   I. Title.
HQ801.M414   1997
646.7'7—dc21   97-20048
                                                         CIP

First St. Martin's Griffin Edition: October 1997

10 9 8 7 6 5 4 3 2 1

*"Using a line on someone isn't being dishonest—
merely civilized."*
—ANONYMOUS

Contents

Acknowledgments

I want to thank my wonderful editor (and commiserating comrade in the Dating Wars), Marian Lizzi, for her encouragement and support; similar kudos must go to my supersmart agent, Elizabeth Kaplan. I am also enormously grateful to all the people who were gracious and brave enough to share with me the intimate details of their love life—I wish I could thank each person by name, but *you know who you are.*

Last but not least, to all the men I've ever dated: Thanks, guys, for all the great material.

Come-Ons,
Comebacks,
AND
Kiss-Offs

Introduction

ON KISSING FROGS

t seemed promising.

He was well educated (Yale/Columbia) and not at all bad-looking. He was exceedingly civil to the waiter and courteous to me; in fact, his manners were unusually impeccable. It was our first date, and even though I absolutely loathe first dates, I had made up my mind to try not to be overly critical. Okay, so he *didn't* have a lot of money. (I've never been the gold digger type, especially during a single man shortage.) And, sure, he *was* working as a temp. (Presumably he wouldn't always be. That's why they call it "temp," right?) I even decided to be open-minded about what he described to me as an unrealized ambition for a career in the field of podiatry. (So what's wrong with feet?) All in all, things were going well enough for me to begin to entertain the possibility of a second date.

It was when he started telling me about his Victoria's Secret catalog collection that I began to get a bad feeling. Even then I tried not to panic. "Wait . . . I must have missed something," I told myself. And so for clarification, I asked him, "And you use these catalogs for . . . ?" assuming that he would fill in the blank with something semirespectable like "for my multimedia collages." Instead, he merely presented me with a big, guilty grin.

I began to plan how I might cut this lunch short. Like, *real* short.

"You know," I said, trying hard to act casual, the way you would with someone you've just discovered hasn't been taking his medication, "we should probably get the bill as soon as the food comes—I've got a . . . a . . . meeting I forgot about."

"Um, sure, okay," he agreed, to my immense relief. "I'm kind of anxious to get home anyway."

"Oh?" I responded automatically, preoccupied as I was with trying to figure out a way to get the waiter to bring our food to the table quickly.

"Yeah. Today is Monday. My military hardware magazines usually come on Mondays."

I felt a chill crawl up my spine, and all thoughts of food suddenly evaporated. I stood up. "Actually, I really should be going."

My date gave me a dazed look. "But your omelette hasn't come yet."

"I know," I replied, gathering up my purse and preparing to make a run for it. "I'm sorry, but I suddenly remembered some important papers I need to Xerox before the meeting."

"Wait—" He started to fumble with his knapsack. "I'll go with you. I need to run off some copies of my manifesto . . . Hey, wait . . ."

I bolted out of the restaurant, took a circuitous route home, and vowed I'd never go out on another date as long as I lived.

But of course I did.

*T*here's an old saying: You've got to kiss a lot of frogs to find your prince. As psychologically troublesome as this fairy tale–inspired metaphor is (especially since the evolved, modern woman is supposed to have given up looking for her prince and is instead searching for . . . well, just for a nice, sane frog), it in many ways characterizes perfectly the awkward, nerve-wracking, and sometimes humiliating process known as Dating. The truth is, going on a date with a man you don't know very well can be so strange and uncomfortable that it is not entirely *unlike* having to kneel down in the mud, catch a greenish-brown amphibian, and make it hold still while you kiss it. And although very few dates resemble the horror story portrayed above, the really frustrating thing about dating is that most of the time, not only does the frog *not* turn into a prince, he croaks something unintelligible or offensive at you and slips back into the vast and murky Dating Pond.

Indubitably, some women are lucky enough to find their mates without having to dabble much in the world of dating. (And I hate every one of them.) They trip over the man of their dreams while waiting for a bus and fall instantly in love, or they work side by side with their husbands-to-be at the office and their relationships grow naturally. The rest of us, however, are more or less forced to stumble our way through the undignified landscape of clumsy first phone calls, stiff dinner conversations, rejected passes, nervous leave-takings, and all the other embarrassing or confusing moments that go along with dating. And although occasionally you may date someone with whom you feel immediately comfortable, often the onus of being on a "date" can make conversation feel like lifting heavy weights or being stuck in glue. Let's face it. You probably don't know each other very well; you may not have anything in common; and furthermore, there hangs over both of you the subtle or not-so-subtle pressure of expectation. (Does he like me? Do I like him? Am I going to see him again? Will I ever be flossing in front of him?) It's enough to shake anyone's conversational confidence.

Of course, not *all* dates are stressful or unpleasant. Many are actually fun. (I heard a rumor that some even lead to long-term relationships.) But there is an audition quality to most dates—especially first dates—which can be unsettling and exhausting. Invariably, one person likes the other more; as a result, most of these social shopping expeditions will sooner or later end in either your rejecting the date or the date rejecting you. In other words, you can almost always expect at least a minor pang of either Postdate Guilt or Postdate Pain.

If all this weren't enough to keep you home watching Nick at Night, today's wild new world of electronic personals, E-mail relationships, gender bending, and (as we are never for one, single, solitary second *ever* allowed to forget) sexually transmitted diseases has made the dating and mating scene totally bewildering. Unlike in the days of arranged marriages and formalized courtship rituals, there are no rules. Who calls whom? Who pays? Who makes the first move? Who proposes the next date? What does it mean when you get invited over to his place for dinner? If he's had three marriages and no therapy is he an automatic throwback? And how do you politely communicate to him that he's not really your cup of cappuccino?

Now, I have been on many dates in my life. (I won't say *how* many. That privileged information is stashed away with my weight and the exact amount of my Visa card debt.) And okay, I confess I haven't *always* had the right thing to say to fill every uncomfortable silence. I certainly don't *perpetually* produce the perfect comeback to every witticism or criticism. But when I do, it is extremely satisfying. There is nothing quite like coming up with the right line for the right moment. Getting off a good line, for example, after someone you've only known for forty-five minutes tells you that you must have been *really* pretty when you were young, can mean the difference between feeling pulverized or victorious.

In the pages that follow, I have attempted to present the world's best and most useful date lines. These questions, quips, comments, and comebacks cover almost every conceivable dating circumstance, from pickups to kiss-offs, and range from the polite to the outrageous. There are simple filling-the-silence lines and don't-get-too-personal deflecting lines. There are wisecracks for dealing with wisecrackers, balance-throwing questions for getting the upper hand, and soothing-the-savage-beast lines for psychos and sex-only seekers. There are all types of flattery lines, as well as test lines for various date situations. There are date-escape lines and lines for other emergencies. There are even multipurpose lines that can work well as tests, subject changers, tension diffusers, or smoke screens.

Having an appropriate date line at your figurative fingertips can help you move through your dating experiences with greater dignity and make you a more confident player in the game of romance. Maybe the next time that man you've been making eyes at all night launches your heart into your esophagus by actually approaching you, you'll be ready with an intriguing response. And when the dweeb your boss set you up with calls you for the fifth time, you'll know just how to politely make sure there isn't a sixth. You might even be prepared to effectively counteract the unexpected silence that descends right after you suggest to your newfound love interest that you'd really like to see him again sometime.

Each date on which you can look back without cringing at something you did or didn't say will help keep your attitude optimistic about the whole, crazy, ego-exposing crapshoot. So what if you use a line somebody else thought up? The minute you say it, it becomes your own. And you certainly don't want to be tempted to forego the mating dance altogether just because you are afraid you won't know the steps.

At one point, after a series of excruciatingly bad dates, I myself renounced dating. I decided it was totally uncool and even psychologically unhealthy to put myself "on the market" and go through these intrusive, intimidating, interminable, interviewlike interactions. I simply swore off dates and spent my spare time trying to psychically manifest a man—solely through meditation and affirmation (not to mention a few candles and crystals). He would be romantic, robust, and red-bearded; he would love dolphins, ballroom dancing, and poker. He would be tolerant of my family, charming with my friends, and completely in love with me. And, best of all, it would be love at first sight. No clumsy questions, no wading through the mundane details of each others lives, no wondering if he'll call.

Then one day an old friend phoned me. "Are you over your date phobia yet?"

"What do you mean?" I demanded, a little defensively. "I'm working on myself, on the inner me; the rest will take care of itself."

"Oh, baloney," said my friend. "Are you ready to get back in there or what?"

"Certainly not," I huffed. "I'm not going to parade myself in front of strange men like some desperate—"

"*Look.* He's thirty-eight, an architect, divorced for two years, no kids, has all his hair and teeth and a house in Duchess County. You want him or not? I've got others on the list."

Well, gentle reader, that was that. I was dating once again.

Chapter One:

PERFECTING THE PICKUP

To attract men, I wear a perfume called
"New Car Interior."
—RITA RUDNER

he first time anyone tried to pick me up was
when I was twelve. My older sister and I were
strolling along the Rehoboth Beach boardwalk,
looking for adventure, when two foreign-
looking boys approached us. They introduced themselves
and told us they were from Iran. (In my twelve-year-old
brain, this evoked vague images of turbans, harems, and
belly dancing.)

"You girls are very pretty," one of the boys said, "and we
are very strangers here." My sister and I giggled nervously.

After walking with us a little bit, the other boy inquired
politely, "Would you like to take a bath with us tomorrow?"

I'm not sure the two young men ever realized just why it
was that my sister and I ran squealing off into the night
(After all, what was so funny about asking two girls to go for
a swim on a public beach?), but we never forgot them—even
though the encounter probably lasted no more than five or six

minutes. It wasn't just the exotic (for us) nature of the two Iranians that made it so memorable; there is something innately powerful about the experience of sparring romantically with strangers.

Indeed, whether you call it "mingling," "a date with destiny," or "cruising the meat market," there is no aspect of human interaction that has been given more attention than The Pickup. From chance meetings in bookstores in Woody Allen films to beach bimbo bagging on *Baywatch,* pickup scenes are continually portrayed in every area of our media culture. And in particular, people seem peculiarly and perpetually preoccupied with pickup *lines.* And though it is certainly an alluring idea that magic words exist that automatically open the door to sexual pleasure or romantic fulfillment, the real reason for the emphasis on opening lines is this: When meeting strangers, especially in a crowd, there is not a whole heck of a lot of time for you even to get the other person's attention, much less let the person know anything about who you are. You are under great pressure to—in one or two sentences—somehow hook the person before they swim away again, destined to nibble at someone *else's* line.

Deep down most of us still believe in the idealistic notion that somewhere out there, waiting in the mist, is our soul mate, our true love, the man of our dreams—if only we knew what in the world to say to him when we meet him.

The Cool Cat: Subtle Pickup Lines

Many women feel that using a pickup line on a man makes them look too aggressive, that women should be like cats (aloof) and men like dogs (panting and eager), and that most males—even today—still like to believe *they* are doing the chasing. These women will attempt to attract the man non-verbally and make *him* use a line on *them*. However, if you prefer to take a little more active role and give Cupid a nudge, don't worry: There *are* ways for you to make the first move without having to throw your arms around the guy's neck and tell him you want to have his baby.

The subtle approach requires that you place yourself in proximity to your target before employing your line. (Although subtle lines are really not lines at all.) It's important that it at least *appear* as though you had not thought of talking to the guy until after you are standing or sitting near him. But don't forget to smile, or your subtle forward pass may sail right over his head.

DATE LINES

"I just love this place [view/bartender/painting]."

"I'm very interested to know what other people think of this event [meeting/reading/music]. Do you mind my asking you?"

(Glancing sideways at him) "So, what's *your* story, anyway?"

(If he is reading a newspaper) "So, what's in the news today? Is the world still turning?"

"Wow! Is it always so hot [smoky/loud/crowded] in here?"

"What *is* that? It looks delicious!" (Warning: This line is to be used only when the man has something to eat or drink in front of him.)

"I'm rather embarrassed to admit this, but I don't know a soul in here."

"Got a light? Thanks. Not too many of us left, are there?" (If you're both smoking, you are such dinosaurs that you're already practically related.)

"I just decided to break the usual rule about talking to strangers. Anyway, you don't look that strange."

"Hi. I'm not the type of woman who usually talks to men I don't know . . . Well, okay, apparently I am!"

"Is this seat taken?" (A trusty old standby.)

"Do you think the bartender sees me?" (Look helpless and thirsty.)

"I'm looking for an opening line. Do you have any suggestions?"

Using Subterfuge

I once heard about a bizarre woman who, hoping to meet and marry a doctor, would actually stage a pickup drama. (Her father was a doctor, but I'll skip the psychological guesswork. Hopefully she has gotten some therapy by now.) She would get dressed to the nines, walk into a bar or cafe near a hospital, and promptly faint dead away on the floor. When she heard the inevitable "Is there a doctor in the house?" it was music to her ears. The idea was that the physician of her dreams would come to her rescue, and after she was "revived" (whereupon she would offer fatigue or extreme hunger as the reason for her saloon swoon), said physician would succumb to her charms. Of course, the doctor could be the wrong sex or could just help her to a seat and go back to his onion soup. But either way, she succeeded in immediately locating the MDs in the crowd, and at the same time, brought herself— if somewhat weirdly—to their attention. While she risked public embarrassment, her romantic ego was safe (as long as her Camille act was not discovered).

Now, as much as I believe in the friendly fib, I would never advocate going as far as the doctor-seeking fainter. On the other hand, an acquaintance of mine (I'll call him Jeff) told me a wonderful—and much more practical—subterfuge pickup story. It happened one night when he was waiting for the subway. He was on his way home from a catastrophically bad blind date when a nice-looking woman approached him. Smiling, she sidled up to him and said, "Excuse me, do you know if the N train goes to Forty-second Street?"

Now, this took place in New York City. Jeff could tell this woman was no tourist (New Yorkers have a certain look about them—a sort of relaxed tenseness), and there isn't a New Yorker alive who doesn't know that *all* subway trains stop at Forty-second Street. And so Jeff's response to the woman was a warm but slightly derisive, "It most certainly does." She thanked him, after which conversation was easy.

Of course, the woman *knew* that he knew that she knew that the N train stopped at Forty-second Street. And so, under the guise of a simple request for information, the following message was plainly but gently delivered: "You look like an interesting man; I might like to get to know you." Best of all, because the woman's approach was cloaked in a request for directions, it could have been easily rebuffed, with both people's egos remaining intact.

P.S. It wasn't rebuffed. Believe it or not, Jeff and the subway stranger were married two years later. (And if you think I'm making this up, just ask me how often I've been talking to strangers on the subway lately.)

DATE LINES

"I'm so sorry to bother you, but could you tell me where you got that briefcase [umbrella/pen/etc.]? I have been dying to get something just like it."

"Excuse me—have you seen a man with a red beard [in a tuxedo/wearing a fedora]? I was supposed to meet a friend; I'm afraid he may not be coming." (If he likes what he sees he's bound to offer to keep you company.)

"I have had the world's *worst* day. You, on the other hand, look like your day wasn't so bad. Won't you tell me about it so I can live vicariously?"

"Can you help me? There's someone here who has been harassing me. I hate to impose, but would you mind talking to me for a few minutes so he won't come back?" (Warning: Don't use this line if you've been sitting conspicuously alone all evening. He'll think you're wacko.)

"Excuse me, I just wanted to thank you for sending me the drink. Oh, you didn't? I'm sorry . . . it must have been some *other* handsome man."

"You have a very strong aura [make up what colors you see], which tells me you are sensual, self-confident—and that you desperately want to have a drink with me."

"I came over to ask you what time it was . . . but suddenly, I don't seem to care."

"Didn't I meet you on a hot and sultry night in New Orleans last year?"

(Bumping into him and spilling something) "Oh! Excuse me, I am so clumsy. I can't believe this! Can I buy you a drink, or a new suit or something?"

(Sotto voce) "Excuse me, I hate to bother you, but someone just bet me that I wouldn't just walk up to you and talk to you—no, don't look! You'd be doing me a really big favor if you'd pretend to find me fascinating."

The Sledgehammer: Blatant or Outrageous Openings

We have all heard the smarmy pickup lines men like to brag about using, such as, "Are those pants mirrored? Because I can see myself in them," but if they ever tried one on me, I'd run screaming into the night. These kinds of lines, while touted as pickup lines, seem like flat-out insults to me (or at least signs of severe immaturity), and even when delivered by a woman to a man are pretty tacky.

However, I *have* heard some outrageous approaches that occasionally work. My favorite—recounted to me by my friend Harvey but never attempted by me (not yet, anyway)—is to go up to a man and simply say firmly, "Get your coat. We're leaving." (Though I think this may have worked better in the seventies than it would now.)

If you are ready to go way out on a limb (and risk having the guy cut the limb completely off your tree, rejection-wise), then I heartily encourage you to be brave and try one or more of the following "do or die" date lines. When they do work, they work amazingly well. You never know: One day—long after you have found that much written-about, much-coveted relationship—your man may turn to you and say, "Honey, I'll never forget when we first met and you said ————. I think I knew right then that you were the one for me!"

DATE LINES

"Excuse me, you remind me of someone I used to know. Except . . . I think you're even better looking."

"*Please* tell me you are single [straight]!"

"If you are married or gay I swear I'll kill myself."

"I never approach strange men, but for you I'm making an exception."

"Well, hello there. I *knew* today was my lucky day."

(Giving him the once-over) "You know, I had just decided to give up on men forever. Now I see I may have to revise that position."

"I was thinking of trying to pick you up [pause, smile] but I may not be strong enough."

"Wow. Where did *you* come from? Heaven?"

"Are you a hologram? You can't be real."

"Excuse me. I just want to know if you are this attractive in the daytime."

"Hi. Are you waiting for someone or are you here to keep me company [buy me a drink/cup of coffee]?"

"I think I dreamt about you last night. No wonder I woke up smiling."

"I'm sorry if this seems forward, but I have never seen a man with such incredible eyelashes. They're so long! (Note: Men tell me this is a great compliment. But do make sure he's not in drag.)

"Mmmmm, just when I thought my day couldn't get any better."

"Are you here alone, she said hopefully?"

"Haven't I seen you in a commercial?"

. "So where've I been all your life, anyway?"

"I think I've seen you somewhere . . . maybe it was in some lovely [exciting/nice/hot/wet] dream I had."

"*God,* I love men in tuxedoes."

"I was thinking of asking you for the time, but I'd rather have your phone number."

"If you don't talk to me, it will ruin my day."

"May I buy you a drink? Or maybe a BMW?" (And if he says, "I'll take the BMW," you say, "Well, sit down and let's talk colors!")

The Classic Approach: Famous First Lines

I am a big believer in cliches, *when used consciously.* They can serve as safe signposts when you are in unknown social territory. Like proverbs, cliches and other recognizable bon mots provide social and cultural context. I favor movie lines in particular, because using a well-known line from a movie—if the other person recognizes it—establishes specific common conversational ground. When used with a quirky smile or an ironic raising of the eyebrows, a classic opening line can create a nice, familiar feeling, a sense of camaraderie. The classic line says, Isn't this kind of situation so typically uncomfortable that it's funny?

DATE LINES

(Remember: These lines should only be uttered with a definite twinkle in your eye.)

"Haven't we met somewhere before?"

"Of all the gin joints in all the world, you have to walk into mine . . ."

"So, what's a guy like you doing in a place like this?"

"Come here often?"

"Excuse me but, *You look mahvelous!*" (à la Billy Crystal from *Saturday Night Live*)

(If he has pulled out your chair, passed you a coaster, or handed you the happy hour peanuts) "Thanks. I have always depended on the kindness of strangers."

"I think this is the beginning of a beautiful friendship."

"Wuz you ever bit by a dead bee?" (This one will be totally lost on any man who hasn't seen *To Have or Have Not,* but if he hasn't, who needs him?)

BODYTALK

Never forget that your body does a lot of its own talking. "Your lips may say no-no, but your eyes say yes-yes!" (Of course, what's worse is when your lips say yes-yes and your body says no-no.) Here is a brief and completely unscientific guide:

THE MOVE	THE MEANING
Staring (or eye contact that is held just a little too long)	Come hither. or My god, you're handsome!
Winking	Hey, you cutie. or Only you and I understand. or Help, I've got something in my eye.
The raised eyebrow One brow	Oh, *really?* or Wow, I like what I see!
Two brows .	Baby, are you for real? or No way!
Playing with a necklace or dangle earring	I feel sensuous tonight. or I'm bored/looking for someone or something to amuse me. or I'd like more jewelry and I'm willing to do pretty much anything to get it.

THE MOVE	THE MEANING
Playing with hair (this includes the Sweep, the Toss, and the Twirl, as well as general poofing or finger-combing)	I feel girlish and I hope I look alright; I want you to like me! or I'm nervous, narcissistic, and/or deeply insecure. or I have cooties.
Staring into drink or off into space	Something tragic has happened to me. or I'm trying really hard to look mysterious or intense.
Running a fingertip around the rim of a glass	Fellah, you should see me in bed.
Fussing with fingernails	I've given up on meeting anyone; I'm going to use this time to clean my nails.

(Caution: Using two or more of the above body signals at the same time may be interpreted as "I'm so neurotic I'm twitching all over the place.")

Chapter Two

COMEBACKS TO COME-ONS

No matter how love-sick a woman is, she shouldn't take the first pill that comes along.
—DR. JOYCE BROTHERS

ou may think you'd rather die than make the first move, but responding to the man's opening line can be harder than delivering the first line yourself. Nervousness or surprise (or sometimes, unfortunately, repugnance)—along with the pressure you may feel to produce a witty comeback—can completely derail your brain, causing calamity. I know of one woman who, in answer to a dashing stranger's provocative "Are you here with someone, angel?" was horrified to hear herself reply bitingly, "My name's not Angel." What she had intended was a sexy "Believe me, I'm no angel." Alas, it was too late; the man went on to graze in a greener—and less confusing—pickup pasture.

Green Light: When You're Interested

Okay. Suddenly, there he is, standing in front of you. He has spoken to you and is leaning against the bar, an appreciative, quizzical look on his face. You are pretty sure you like the cut of his jib. What do you do now?

Our grandmothers, as well as certain neotraditionalist books like *The Rules,* would more than likely advise playing hard to get. This prevaricative practice stems from the assumption that men are prey—to be sneakily snagged, bagged, tricked, caught, or hog-tied—and that they will never want to get anything that they think wants to get *them.* Well, I grew up on Doris Day movies too, but even I hold the somewhat more moderate view that it's not so much about playing hard to get as it is about (especially in the beginning) keeping him guessing. In other words, if a man should approach you and tell you you look like a million dollars, it may be better to say, "You're at least a hundred yourself," than, "Thanks, you gorgeous hunk, you look like a man I could set up house with."

Like other kinds of faux pas, mistakes in this area can easily happen when you are stressed out or have overimbibed. I am ashamed to admit that once, after I had absorbed two large martinis, a waiter/actor asked me if I thought he was attractive enough for films, and I exclaimed much too loudly, *"Are you kidding? You're a God!"*

DATE LINES

 ### TO THE COMPLIMENT
("Do you know how beautiful you are?")

"No. Why don't you tell me?"

"I bet you say that to all women who are about to buy you a drink [a cappuccino]."

(Dismissively) "Oh, go on." (Then enthusiastically) "No really, *go on!*"

"Hmmm. Is that a gun in your pocket or are you trying to kill me with flattery."

 ### TO OFFERS OF REFRESHMENTS
("Can I buy you a drink?")

"I thought you'd never ask."

"No, but I'll buy *you* one."

"No, but you can keep me company while I buy *myself* one."

"No, but you can buy me dinner."

TO QUERIES ABOUT YOUR BEING UNACCOMPANIED

("Excuse me, are you here alone?")

"Not anymore, it seems."

"As a matter of fact, I am. Would you care to alter the situation?"

(Musingly) "Is anyone ever really alone?"

"Actually, I'm here with a huge rabbit named Harvey."

TO SUGGESTIONS OF RECOGNITION

("I think I may have seen you here before.")

"Probably not. I definitely would have remembered *you*."

"I hope so. I like to be seen as much as possible."

"Perhaps you've seen me in your dreams; I've seen you in mine."

TO THE QUESTION "WHAT DO YOU DO?"

(A lot of people use this as an opening line, even though it is a real clunker. You can, of course, answer this one straight, as in, "I'm an advertising executive." But it may move things in a more playful direction if you adopt one of the stances below.)

The Tough Gal: "Whatever I want."

The Seductress: "Whatever you want."

The Cool Customer: "As little as possible."

The Challenger: "What do you *think* I do?"

The Philosopher: "It's not so much what a person does as much as what she is."

MISCELLANEOUS COMEBACKS
(You never know when one of these will fit the bill—or the Tom, Dick, or Harry)

"You know, I've heard that men are from Mars but for you I might be willing to relocate."

"You're married? That's okay, I've been looking for a husband."

"I'm *not* that kind of girl . . . but I might be that kind of woman!"

"If you are going to try to pick me up, please don't let me fall for you."

Red Light: Lines for Discouraging Lushes, Lechers, and Other Less-Than-Desirables

Not too long ago I was out walking, contentedly mulling over some idea or other in my head, when suddenly a man's voice hissed in my ear, "Oooh, baby, nice asssss!" Unpleasantly jolted and thoroughly annoyed, I was not surprised to find myself looking into the leering face of a strange male. Naturally, I did what most of us do in this situation: I ignored him and kept walking. But here's my fantasy response:

I stop, dig into my purse, and come up with a small calling card with printing on it. Smiling, I hand the offending man the card. He stares at me in disbelief, naturally assuming I am giving him my phone number. I walk quickly away, leaving him peering at the card.

All the card has on it, in very small letters, is this:

> *If I wanted your opinion on any part of my anatomy,*
> *I would have asked for it, you pea brain.*

(Please don't actually try this. I have been driven to this kind of warped fantasy by years of living in New York City.)

All too often the man who decides to present himself to you is obnoxious, insulting, drunk, a fascist, not your type, clearly only interested in sex, married, or all of the above; even though most of the time he's not accosting you on the street but is merely sitting next to you somewhere. And sometimes the man may not be so much unappetizing as he is just in the way of your meeting more eligible men. So how can you get these unwanted fellows to go away and leave you alone?

Thanks to twisted social conditioning (where hard-to-get is considered a common female ploy and "No" means "Show me how much you want me, baby") and the existence of testosterone, men often see discouraging remarks from a female the way a bull sees a red cape. This is why sometimes an unappealing yes can work better than a clever no, and many times silence and a cold look—followed by the back of your head—is the best way to handle a truly obnoxious suitor. (If he's drunk, there's usually no use in even trying to dissuade him. The best course of action is to trick him. Tell him you have something very contagious, like mono, or ask him if he has an extra glass for you to put your teeth in.) And always remember that when all stop signs fail to have an effect, you may be forced simply to remove yourself from charging distance.

 DATE LINES

("What's a pretty little lady like you doing here?")

"Hoping to be left alone. Do you mind?" (Smile politely.)

"Waiting for you, sweetie! But you know, you don't look like the kind of guy who would be *interested* in a man in drag."

("What are you drinkin', babe? Lemme buy you one.")

"No thank you. I never accept drinks from men I don't intend to talk to."

"Thanks but my next two drinks are already paid for in advance."

"Oh yes, *do* buy me a drink. Drinking helps my yeast infection."

"Yes, do buy me one; maybe after more alcohol even you might seem charming."

("You certainly are beautiful.")

"Thanks, my husband thinks so too."

"You should have seen me before my plastic surgery."

"Stop staring at my breasts or I'll spray you with silicone."

("You here all by your lonesome?")

"I'm alone, but not lonesome."

"Well, I *was* with that lovely woman over there, but then she told me she was incredibly attracted to you and was hoping you'd come and talk to her, so I decided to make myself scarce."

("Haven't I seen you somewhere before?")

"I seriously doubt it."

"Impossible; I just got out of prison yesterday."

"Maybe. I *have* been on TV recently—as a spokeswoman for the gay women's movement."

("So, what do you do?")

"What makes you think I *do* anything?

"Nothing that would interest you."

("So, what's your sign?")

"Do Not Enter"

("My place or yours?")

"Both: You go to your place and I'll go to mine."

("Can I call you?")

"Sure, but don't expect me to answer."

If you are being pawed, pinched, or otherwise manhandled:

"Excuse me, you're on private property."

"Sir, do I look like a curtain rod?" ("What d'ya mean?" "Because you're hanging all over me.")

"What do you think I am, a grapefruit?"

"You can look, but don't touch."

"Who gave *you* the keys to the city?"

General repellents

"What part of 'no' don't you understand?"

"I'm afraid you're just not my cup of arsenic."

"Wow. Have you actually had any success with that line?"

"Listen, buddy, you're barking up the wrong tree. In fact, you're in the wrong yard."

"I'm sure there is less of you than meets the eye."

"Frankly, my dear, I don't give a damn."

"Listen, doll-face, why don't you do us all a favor and go back to your home planet?"

Yellow Light: The Art of Ambiguity

There may be times when you do not want to commit to either a yes *or* a no. That is, you may not want to exactly encourage the guy, but neither are you ready to send him packing. Barbara, one woman I interviewed, recounted an incident in which she was paired up with an amorous business client at an awards ceremony. She took an immediate dislike to him, but for obvious reasons was not in a position to give him the verbal heave-ho. She resorted instead to the fine art of ambiguity; that is, she continually countered his come-ons with lines like, "Well, aren't you *something.*"

The beauty of ambiguity is that it allows you to stay comfortably seated on the fence. It is useful not only when you are forced to hide your true feelings, like Barbara was, but also when you are not sure what your feelings may be. It's a sort of stalling strategy. Ambiguous lines are ones that make him think to himself, "Huh?" (As usual, some of these lines will suit you better than others. Pick one that fits your personality and use it when you are feeling confused or noncommittal—or just want to keep him guessing.)

DATE LINES

"You know, it's men like you who make the world what it is."

"As men go—oh, boy!"

"You certainly have some interesting ideas about things."

"I'm not one of those women who is going to go on and on about how wonderful you are." (smile)

"Did you know that a kiss is an anatomical juxtaposition of two orbicular muscles in a state of contraction?"

"When God closes a bore, he opens a bimbo." (This of course makes no sense, but it sounds good and will confuse him.)

"All I know is, it only takes one sip of wine to tell whether or not it's a good bottle."

Quick Getaways

On the other hand, sometimes enough is enough (or too much), and you find yourself praying for someone to just beam you out of there, fast. If you are at a New Year's Eve party and it's 11:50 P.M. and the man who has you cornered has either just begun to tell you about his sinus blockages or about his black satin sheets, you may need to resort to a quick getaway.

DATE LINES

(Instructions: deliver line and skedaddle.)

"Oh! I think I just lost a filling! Excuse me."

"I have to go find my bodyguard."

"I feel really sick."

"Hold on—don't go away, I'll be right back (turn and smile) . . . now you stay *right there* and wait for me!"

"I think my wig is slipping. Will you excuse me while I go straighten it?"

"Sorry—you've made me think of something I have to look up [check on] right away."

Chapter Three:

BLIND DATES

*Be careful of your thoughts; they may become words
at any moment.*
—IARA GASSEN

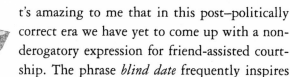t's amazing to me that in this post–politically
correct era we have yet to come up with a non-
derogatory expression for friend-assisted courtship. The phrase *blind date* frequently inspires
snickers and jokes about Seeing Eye dogs. The expression
being fixed up is not much better; after all, you can't be fixed
up unless you have in some way broken down. (Not only
that, but a third party has been forced to step in to do your
fixing *for you.* You had your chance, babe, now step aside and
let someone else give it a whirl.) Even more alarming is the
term *setup,* which implies that you are somehow being
conned. (Wait, don't go! It's a setup, an ambush, a trap!)

The whole concept of blind dating has a (mostly unjus-
tified) dishonorable tinge to it. For one thing, it is presumed
that blind dates are resorted to only after one has exhausted
one's own supply of men. (Or maybe it's because you would
have to be blind to go out with the guy. Ha, ha.) In any case,

blind dates are always a gamble—the grab bag of the dating scene. No matter what your fix-you-up friend tells you, you don't really know what you are getting until you get there.

Luckily, all this bad press on fix-ups is counteracted by the ever-prevalent, intoxicating blind date myth: "Well, my *dear,* a friend of my cousin's met her husband on a *blind date;* can you believe it?" (There would be no treasure hunters if there were no rumors of sunken ships.) As a result, most women I know are happy to be fixed up by their friends.

Remember: Even if your date steps on your foot and talks about flyswatters all evening, you should always thank your friend(s) for arranging a blind date. But don't assume just because it's a setup that the guy isn't an ax murderer. I know someone whose mother got tipsy while on vacation in the Bahamas and gave her daughter's phone number to the man next to her at the bar, with instructions that he call the unsuspecting daughter when he got back to the States. I never found out exactly what was wrong with the man, but the daughter ended up getting an unlisted phone number, which she to this day refuses to give her mom.

Moral: Sometimes friends of friends can be stranger than strangers.

How to Get Your Friends to Cough Them Up

It was when I was talking to my friend Margaret for the seventeenth time about setting me up with a colleague of her husband's that it struck me: Blind dates are often dreaded more by the setter-uppers than they are by the setups them-selves. One result of this reluctance is that single women can spend many frustrating hours listening to descriptions of men they never get to meet.

Margaret had been dangling this particular guy, a col-league of her husband's, in front of me for weeks, and to tell you the truth it was beginning to feel as though I were in some insidious kind of torture chamber.

"I thought about it some more and he's not really your type," Margaret announced. "He's much too serious."

"Look," I responded tiredly, "is the guy single and straight?"

"You probably would have nothing in common."

"I'll tell you what," I said, exasperated, "just give him my phone number and give me his, then we'll have *that* in com-mon." Margaret's husband, who happened to be passing by just then, decided to pipe in helpfully with "He doesn't make enough money."

"I don't give a $#@*! about money!" I practically yelled. "Don't you guys get it? I just want to go on a date once every century or so. When you're thirty-five, single, and living in New York City, your goal isn't to get a rich man, it's to find someone to go to the movies with!"

Lisa and her husband laughed at that and seemed to re-lent at last. "Okay," Margaret said, "we'll set it up."

"*Finally.* Good." I felt as though I had been through a major battle, but it looked as if I had won. Relieved, I started thinking about how I would call my sister on Sunday and tell her I actually had a date. She'd be incredulous at first—

"Wait a minute," Margaret said suddenly, turning to her husband. "Sweetie, isn't he the one who when we fixed him up with Sheryl he took her to that restaurant where she thinks she got food poisoning? Yes, that *was* him. We can't poison another of our friends. Sorry, forget it."

I covered my face with a sofa cushion and screamed.

It can be demoralizing enough to admit you want help getting dates, but having to beg people for them is crushing beyond belief. People do seem to think that if they set two of their friends up on a date, they are responsible for what happens afterwards. They figure that there is a very good chance that *someone* is going to be mad at them afterwards. This boundary problem may be partly counteracted by using one of the following lines with reticent matchmakers.

DATE LINES

"Don't worry. Right now I'm looking for a date, not a mate."

"The question is would we have a nice time at the movies together, not should I have his children."

"I promise you that as long as he doesn't hit me or steal my purse, you get a gold star just for making the introduction."

"Okay, how much do you want for his phone number?"

Phone Lines: The Predate Conversation

Rrrrrrrnnnnggg.

"Hello?"

"Frank . . . I mean, Fred . . . Fred Freemont?"

"Yes, this is Fred."

"Oh . . . Hi . . . this is Susan."

"Uh . . . Susan?"

"I'm sorry. Susan *Jones*. Julie Lippincott's friend? She told me to . . . I mean, she thought you might . . . I mean . . ."

"Oh, yes, *Susan,* sure. Nice to hear from you."

"Yes, well . . . So, Julie tells me you're in real estate?"

(Long pause) "No."

"You're not? Oh, god, I've got the wrong . . ." (sound of shuffling papers) "Sorry. I meant to say you were in graphic design."

"That's right. And tell me, what is it again that *you* do?"

"Me? Why, I'll do just about anything!" (giggle) "Fred? Are you there? Sorry, that was a joke. Actually I'm between things right now, sort of freelancing, here and there. Anyway . . . I thought, that is, Julie thought . . . well, would you like to join me in a cup of coffee somewhere, that is, somewhere we'll both fit?" (giggle)

"Um . . . uh . . . actually, I've got a really busy schedule this month."

"Oh . . . you do? Well, that's okay . . . I mean so do I . . . I only wanted to . . . it was only because Julie . . ."

"Hey, Susan? Buh-*bye!*"

Click.

*C*alling a man you don't know can be more terrifying than skydiving over a live volcano. Usually the man will call you first (sexist as it may seem); even so, it can be one of the hardest and most awkward conversations you'll ever have. Both people are acutely aware that at least one of you is looking for love and couldn't find it among your acquaintances. Let's face it: Blind date situations are not the most natural situations in the world, and unless you are in better than average psychological health, it can be difficult to maintain your composure.

Even semiself-confident people sometimes need scripts for pre–blind date phone calls. In any case, try not to giggle until *he* says something funny.

 DATE LINES

Tread carefully

"Did Sally tell you I would be calling?"

"Would you be interested in getting together?"

Pave the way with flattery

"I hear you are one of the world's greatest chefs [intellectuals/Rollerbladers/yodelers]."

"I don't go on many blind dates, but after Sally told me about you I thought you should be one of them."

If you want to flirt a little:

"Hold on a second, I just got out of the shower."

Humorous banter is risky on a first phone call; always wait for a cue before using:

"I'm not used to talking to strange men on the phone. Except of course for obscene phone calls."

"Let's meet for coffee. That way, if we bore each other, we'll still have a caffeine high."

"Oh, the museum will be fun. I haven't been to one since I was released from the asylum."

Your First Date Kit

The moment has arrived. There's no turning back; it's time to meet your blind date in the flesh. You open the door to the cafe, feeling at once ridiculous and terrified.

He's sitting over there by the espresso machine. Oh no, you think to yourself, that just *can't* be him. Studly looking and highly coiffed, he is dressed in a mauve velour sweat suit. Yikes! Your friend Sarah didn't bother to tell you he was a Tom Jones look-alike. Not that you're closed-minded, but dressed in your pseudo-sixties India-print muumuu, you are just not the kind of woman a Tom Jones type dreams of. He looks up, and you automatically suck in your stomach.

"John?" you greet him, thinking how little he looks like his voice over the phone.

The initial introductions over and your coffee ordered, you stare at this stranger across the small table and suddenly realize you have absolutely nothing to say to him. You have no idea even where to begin. The silence grows and still your tongue is frozen. The only thing alive in your brain is—horribly, bizarrely—the music of Tom Jones! Desperate for a miracle, you open your mouth, praying something semi-normal will come out of it.

"It's, it's not unusual to be loved by anyone." *Oh, god!* (At least you didn't sing it.) He's looking at you as if you had some kind of weird facial tick. You try to backpedal.

"I don't know why I said that. What I meant to say was . . . it's not that unusual to be . . . surprised by anyone. I mean how different people look than how they sound. On the phone, that is."

The rest of the date is a nightmarish blur. One of the negative aftereffects of the experience is that you can never hear a Tom Jones song again without getting a sick feeling.

First dates of any kind have the potential of exploding in your face. But remember, if you're feeling awkward, odds are he is, too. Here are some lines to help put him and you at ease—or at least to fill some conversation holes with something besides "well . . ." or "so . . ."

DATE LINES

"So, how do you know [when did you meet] the inimitable Sarah, anyway?"

"I just *knew* you'd be tall [have red hair/have really cool glasses]." (Make sure your psychic observation is of a positive nature; that is, never say, "I just *knew* you'd be squinty-eyed.")

"So, tell me the story of your life: How many siblings you have, how many places you've lived . . . and how many times you've had to talk about them on dates like this."

"Know what? I hate first dates. Why don't we pretend this is our second date?"

"I seem to be completely tongue-tied tonight; I hope you won't think I'm into bondage." (Okay, this one is a mite risky.)

"I feel as if I already know you, sort of. Certainly any friend of Sarah's is a friend of mine—or at least not an enemy."

"You realize, of course, that we can say only nice things about Sarah to each other, lest one of us squeals."

Easing the Embarrassment: Blind Date Lines and Jokes

Bob, a divorced man, was having his first blind date in several years. His wife had been beautiful but dumb, so Bob had made up his mind, now that he had evolved a little, to try to

BLIND DATES AS A SPECTATOR SPORT

Sometimes one of your friends decides that it would be dandy to have you meet your potential significant other while she and her spouse look on. Whether this is because the man in question isn't really interested in a blind date (and not to know the true purpose of the social engagement) or because your friend is a date voyeur, having witnesses can be a lot of pressure. Not only are you put under a first meeting microscope (so that your friends can say after you've gone, "I can't *believe* she asked Jim that question; no *wonder* she's still single.") but also it is impossible for you to make a quick getaway if you find him more repulsive than slugs. And of course, afterwards, you have to face the inevitable inquiry from your host(s): "Well, did you like him? Has he called you? I thought he liked you a lot. When he put his napkin on your head that way I could *tell* he really liked you."

Naturally, if the matchmaker is a very close friend, there is less risk of being uncomfortable. (Sometimes other people can provide a desirable buffer.) Also, with good friends, it's not difficult to explain to them beforehand that you find having an audience on a date too nerve-wracking. In any case, if an acquaintance insists on a group affair, try telling him you'd be too self-conscious and ask whether the man might not be interested in getting together with you alone—even if it's just for coffee. Say something like, "There are only a few things in life I like to do without an audience: first dates are one of them." Or even, "Why don't you let us have our first dinner alone; we'll have the engagement party at your house."

(P.S. If you do go on one of these setups-disguised-as-innocent-get-togethers, always make sure you know who your designated man is. You could end up unwittingly making eyes at someone else's husband. And that is, in most households, a no-no.)

focus less on looks and more on brains this time around. To that end, a buddy of his had set him up with Gloria, who his buddy claimed was extremely intelligent.

During dinner, Gloria talked nonstop about the Psychic Friends Network. (It was apparent that Gloria called her psychic quite a lot.) Bob tried to change the subject to something more interesting but to no avail. Finally, as they were having dessert, Gloria bubbled, "Bob, you know what? My psychic told me that . . . like . . . that I was going to meet my true soul mate tonight!"

Bob gave her a wry smile as he signaled the waiter for the check. "I'm not surprised," he said. "I think I knew you in a past wife."

*B*lind dates carry such a bad stigma that sometimes a blind date joke can be helpful in dispelling the awkwardness. Now, you have to be careful when trotting out a formal joke like the one above (this one, for example, might strike some people as sexist, insinuating that all women are airheads), but if the man has a sense of humor and doesn't mind a bit of silliness, the following quips can say: Can you believe we're doing this? Are we dweebs or what? Can you believe we agreed to be *set up?*

DATE LINES

"I guess since you accepted a *blind* date you must not be *seeing* anyone."

"Did you know this is my very first blind date? Yours too? Great. Well, now that we've got the lies out of the way . . ."

"For a blind date, you've sure got beautiful eyes."

"This may be a blind date, but I've got my eyes wide open."

(If you should go to a place with very low lighting) "I know this is supposed to be a blind date, but this is ridiculous."

(At the end of the date) "Well, I've got to hurry home and call [name of person who set you up] to report!"

Chapter Four:

PLAYING THE PERSONALS
(OR, MY MOTHER WARNED ME NOT TO
TALK TO STRANGERS BUT FOR YOU I
SEEM TO BE MAKING AN EXCEPTION)

*The best impromptu speeches are the ones written
well in advance.*
—RUTH GORDON

For many women, entering the world of the personals can be traumatic. Ingrained in most of us is a misconception about the methods of meeting men that I call The Dating Tier of Degradation. It goes like this:

THE DATING TIER OF DEGRADATION

1) *Regular or Organic Dating (girl meets boy, then dates boy):* Can be excruciating, but is seen as the natural path to romance. Is universally considered to be socially acceptable.

2) *Blind Dates:* Many people on earth have never had to experience these. They are often regarded as unhip and indicate a certain undignified overeagerness.

3) *The Personals:* One step above blowup dolls.

Thanks in part to the trendy new world of cyberdating, this prejudice against the personals has been greatly diminished. Even my friend Carol finally succumbed to the inevitable. She always used to say that answering a personal ad was like doing heroin: You only tried it if you were feeling really desperate; each experience is exciting for a brief period but when it's over you feel empty or sick; and once you've done it, you can't stop. But at last, at the insistence of all her friends—who convinced her that there were actually great men floating around out there in the personals world—Carol took the plunge.

Her very first date was with a freelance editor who sounded wonderful in his ad and on the phone; he had a wry sense of humor and a sensitive air about him. He was up on new fiction and down on the Moral Majority. He liked the same movies Carol did. He had a bit of a quirky side—he collected marbles—but at least when Carol asked him if he still had all of his, he laughed. As for his appearance, he told her he had long hair and was fairly fit.

They met at a dinner. He looked normal enough, and Carol sat down, somewhat relieved. She started by making what she hoped was an amusing observation about the strange world of the personals, and how it was like a different country with its own special language. Then her date smiled.

To say that he had no teeth would be unfair, as Carol told me after it was all over, but the brutal truth was that his two front teeth were definitely and alarmingly missing. Carol almost dropped her water glass in shock. It wasn't the fact of the missing teeth that bothered her as much as the fact that he seemed to think it quite normal, that it needed no explanation or forewarning. She told me that she was tempted to

ask him just what the deal was: Did they recently get
knocked out in a barroom brawl while he was protecting
some woman's honor? Could he not afford to fix them? Did
it make it easier to drink from a straw? Or did he simply like
the *Hee Haw* look? Though Carol never went out again with
the toothless man, she persevered (after taking a brief hiatus
to recover) in the world of the personals, and eventually met
some interesting men with plenty of good teeth.

I've heard a number of painful personals stories involv-
ing all manner of weirdos—from foot fetishers to transves-
tites. No matter how good your screening process, you can
sometimes end up with an unpleasant surprise. Unfortunately, it's much more likely that he'll be disappointing in
the normal way: boring, obnoxious, sleazy, or obviously un-
interested in you.

What you must always keep in mind when playing the
personals (and this goes for cyberdating as well) is that you
are now in the realm of major frog kissing. It's a numbers
game. In fact, knowing the odds, another friend, Linda, made
up her mind that she would kiss (not literally, of course) no
less than one hundred frogs before giving up her search for a
mate. Guess what? She only had to kiss forty-seven. And
Linda, who is now happily seated on her dream lily pad with
her loving frog prince, will tell you that it was unquestion-
ably worth it.

Rule number one: Enjoy the process. The worst that can
happen is that you end up with a great Date From Hell story
to tell at your next all-women, all-night poker game. And in
the meantime you just may be pleasantly surprised at how
much you learn about men, about dating, and above all,
about yourself.

Please note: This chapter will not cover what to put *in*

your ad. How to write a good personal ad—for example, whether you should physically represent yourself as "willowy," "languorous," "Marilyn Monroe-ish," or "Have Body to Die For"—is a subject that could (and does) fill many books. All I will say here is that it doesn't pay to exaggerate too much when you are describing yourself. People who are using the classifieds have a very buy-and-sell attitude; if you say your car is shiny red and it is in actuality a dingy brown, the man usually won't even bother to look under the hood. (And yes, 99 percent of the male species is more interested in looks than women are. If anyone needs proof, all you have to do is read the personal ads posted by most men in any publication: "42-year-old man looking for pretty, slender, 22-year-old, preferably brunette . . ." This is one of the many reasons it's better to place your own ad rather than answer other people's. Who wants to wade through all that testosterone poisoning?)

Safety First: Screening Tests

As any woman who has played the personals game will tell you, the phone interview is extremely important for weeding out the men who definitely aren't for you (and of course, any stray perverts who may have fallen into the mix). Along with the usual questions that your prospective date will be prepared to answer, such as where do you work, where did you go to school, what part of the city do you live in, have you been married, do you have any kids, or have you ever been ar-

rested, the following questions might just reveal some subtle but important personality/lifestyle information, thereby
saving you time and trouble (not to mention money, if you're
the one paying). For example, if in answer to "Who's your favorite author," the man answers, "The Marquis de Sade," you
might want to think twice.

Be lighthearted with these questions. So that it doesn't
sound like a questionnaire from *The Dating Game,* use only
one or two questions per man, and try to work them into a
natural place in your conversation. And remember, if you *do*
get a funny feeling when you are on the phone with someone,
respect that feeling! You are in strict better-safe-than-sorry
land when you are dealing with the personals. You *will* end
up throwing some good ones out with the bad, but you have
to look at each iffy candidate as you would a week-old piece
of chicken you find in your fridge: Sure, maybe it's okay, but
why take a chance on getting salmonella?

 ## DATE LINES

"How long have you been doing this personals thing?"

"I'm new to this; do you tell people in your life about
your personals dating? Do you only tell a few people? Is it a
complete secret?"

"What's your favorite thing to do in the city [in town/on
the weekends]?"

"Who is your favorite female celebrity?"

"Who's your favorite author?"

"So are you a cat person or a dog person?"
(This is a trick question; it doesn't really matter which one he is. But if he answers "I hate all creatures that walk the earth on four legs," well now, *that* tells you something. Also this query allows him to ask if *you* have any pets; and if he doesn't, it could be a sign of abnormal self-absorption. Yes, I know, with men it *is* hard to tell.)

"What do you think about all this New Age stuff, anyway?" (You may be able to find out from this question whether he is on a spiritual path or he is a cynical atheist, or something in between.)

"If there were a movie made about your life, who do you think they would get to play you?" (If the guy responds with "Pee Wee Herman," "Kramer on *Seinfeld*," or "Bela Lugosi," better make sure he's kidding.)

"Are you more of a coffee-and-morning person, a wine-and-evening person, or a martini-and-late-night person?"

"What did you like best about my ad? [Or, How many responses have you gotten to your ad?]"

"Please excuse my asking, but do you have a major thing for the Three Stooges?"

"Are you a clear-shower-curtain guy or an opaque?"

"Is this your real name?"

THE CALL WAITING ESCAPE

Whether he's exhausting your patience with a detailed account of his ten years of analysis (I don't care what anyone says, there is such a thing as too much therapy), or he's just told you that what he is really looking for is a woman to go to revival meetings with, you may need an easy way to abort the call in a hurry. Although he may suspect the following, commonly used "faux call waiting" escape technique, it's a hard one to prove. The guy will never know for sure. Anyway, it's not quite as cruel as just plain old hanging up on him.

INSTRUCTIONS

Step one: Create the illusion of a call waiting signal by lightly tapping the receiver button. Be careful not to disconnect the person, which can happen if you press down too hard or too long. If you have a dial phone, you can rotate the dial slightly to imitate the call waiting signal. If you live in one of the areas that now have a silent call waiting signal, you can omit this step entirely.

Step two: As if embarrassed or annoyed, interrupt your phone suitor with, "Oh, I'm sorry, can you hold on? It's my call waiting."

Step three: If your phone doesn't have a hold button (many new phones do), place your hand securely over the mouthpiece for approximately fifteen seconds.

Step four: Carefully take your hand off the mouthpiece. Say: "Hi. Listen, I've got to take this. It's long distance [it's my sick grandmother/it's my boss/it's my long-lost daughter]."

Step five: If you don't already have his number, pretend to take it down if he offers it, but *don't* promise to call him back. Hang up quickly.

(Note: If during the procedure you accidentally disconnect your caller, wait until he calls back and then say, "I'm sorry, I think there's something wrong with my phone, I—" and hang up again. Keep doing this until he goes away.)

Lines On-line: About Cyberdating

Over the last two or three years, there have been many stories circulating about people meeting on the Internet or getting engaged by E-mail; I even heard an account of two people getting married via the Net. It all sounded so progressive that I was beginning to feel quite hopeful about the whole cyber-romance business. Then one day I happened to overhear someone talking about a woman he knew who was affianced to someone she had met on the Net *but whom she had never met in the flesh.* The truth is, the more I listen to cyberdaters' stories, the more alarmed I become. People don't seem to realize that while the technologies are different, the cyberdating and personals worlds are essentially the same: *You are dealing with strangers.* Intermingling on the Internet may afford you the comfort of a longer period of anonymity; but don't be fooled by the high-tech hype—you are still advertising for a date or picking up someone you don't know from Adam.

In fact, most cyberspace encounters are *truly* blind dates, as you can't even look into a man's eyes, read his expression, or see whether he is wearing a polyester suit or a tie-dyed dashiki. And while there is certainly an advantage to having a long on-line correspondence before you commit to a face-to-face meeting, during the time you are writing you never get to hear the person's voice. (Voices can reveal a lot about a person.) Cyberspace is a notorious arena for liars. Sitting at home at their computer terminal, people seem to feel disposed to reinvent themselves, to become anyone they want to be on the World Wide Web. Moreover, they have all the time they need to create their persona, since they don't have to send their messages until they are perfected. Men pretend to be women, women pretend to be men, teenagers pretend to be middle-aged, pornographers pretend to be Hollywood movie directors. It's the same weird wacky world that's out there on the street, it's just coming to you through the misleadingly comforting light of your personal monitor. And even if you play it very safe in cyberspace, you can end up wasting a lot of time writing to guys who will never pan out. (C.A.—Cyberspace Anonymous—may be the largest growing twelve-step program in America.)

Nevertheless, for all you super cyberchicks out there, here are some tips: Avoid looking for love in chat rooms, which is a practice tantamount to walking into a bar and talking to every schmuck who happens to be present. (And most chat rooms tend to attract a lot of lowlifes.) Newsgroups are a better place to meet normal, interesting people; however, be aware that newsgroup members may or may not be looking to meet someone. If you do find someone in a newsgroup who interests you, you can investigate him by doing a search of what other newsgroups he may have posted to in the past. (So if, for instance, he's into alt.teen.hygiene, alt.chemical.peel, and alt.MTV.Rancid, you might assume he's under twenty-one. Always remember, there is very little privacy in cyberspace.)

The best place by far to meet potential dates on the Net is— not surprisingly—the personals bulletin boards available through the various Internet providers. The advantages cyberspace does have over running an ad in a newspaper are that you can make your description longer; once you are online the personals service is virtually free; and you can change your description whenever you want. The other big benefit to using the Net is that you can let the computer do what computers are truly meant to do: save you the time and trouble of wading through ads of men whose statistics would eliminate them as candidates for you. In other words, you can search the profiles according to age, race, geographic area, etc.

Cyberspace is the biggest singles party you'll ever go to. *Be careful out there.* And *please* don't fall in love until you see the whites of their eyes.

Some suggestions for on-line lines:

DATE LINES

"How long have you been on the Net? Are you a serious surfer or a newbie?"

"Hey there. What's a guy like you doing in a cyberplace like this?"

"I'm looking for someone to travel down the information superhighway with; but baby, I live life in the exit-only lane."

"Am I misreading you? Is this a nibble or a full-fledged byte?"

"I know I may sound forward, but I want you to know I'm not a woman of easy virtuals."

"Ya wanna come up to my website and see my etchings?"

"How about coming to my private room and checking out my atmospheres?"

"Is that an avatar in your pocket or are you just glad to see me?"

"Did anyone ever tell you you have an attractive profile?"

"So, how big is your hard drive?"

"I bet you've got a real fast modem."

Preparing to Meet: How to Describe Yourself Without Sounding Inane

In arranging to meet my very first personals date, I must admit I was completely caught off guard when—after we had finally decided on a location—the guy asked me, "Well, what do you look like, so I'll know it's you?" Stunned with the sudden realization that I was being called upon to describe myself in a few words without sounding either conceited or insecure, I stammered, "I—I don't know . . . average height, medium brown hair . . . kind of your average woman, I guess."

Most women feel funny giving a physical description of themselves. You may find it easier and more genteel to give a general impression ("People say I look a little like Jodie Foster") rather than a detailed description ("Five foot six, one hundred forty pounds, thirty-seven-and-a-half-inch bust, auburn hair, mole on left shoulder blade . . ."), lest you start to feel like you're your own pimp. I also happen to believe that unless someone is repulsive-looking—and sometimes even then—there is a lot more to chemistry than eye color and bust measurements. On the other hand, if the guy *does* have very specific physical requirements for his potential mate (or playmate, as the case may be), you will want to find this out as soon as possible. Even if you fit his requirements exactly, down to your shoe size, you may not be interested in a man who is that hung up on external qualities.

If, however, there has been no exchange of photographs and you haven't discussed your looks prior to arranging a rendezvous, it is always advisable to have something prepared when you have to answer the inevitable "So how will I recognize you?"

DATE LINES

"Don't worry, I'll find you. I have a sixth sense about these things."

"Me? Oh, I'm a combination of Sophia Loren, Michelle Pfeiffer, and Hillary Clinton." (If you really do look like a combination of famous people, by all means, use it.)

(The sassy retort) "Why, do you have specific requirements?"

"I'll be wearing a red hat and a big smile."

"I'll be wearing a purple scarf, green spiked heels, polka-dot pantyhose, and a patent leather bustier. Oh, hold on . . . that outfit's at the cleaners."

"To tell you the truth, I have no idea what I'll look like tomorrow. Anything could happen."

"I'll let you know after I talk to my hair stylist."

"Oh, you'll recognize me. I'll be the woman with the unmistakable where-is-he-who-is-he look on her face."

The Moment of Truth

I talked with an astounding man named Scott who had been on so many blind dates—and personals dates—he claimed there wasn't anything in the dating universe that he hadn't experienced. One night Scott was sitting at his favorite restaurant, waiting for a woman who had responded to his personal ad. When the maître d' brought her over, she looked familiar to him, but he couldn't quite place her. She sat down, a confused expression on her face.

"Hi, I'm Judy. Do I know you?"

"Yeah," he said. "I'm having a deja vu kind of feeling."

She looked at him hard. "Scott. Scott. Wait, I know . . . it was two years ago, I think you answered my ad."

"Oh, right! God." He groaned. Now he vaguely remembered. They hadn't hit it off, though he couldn't remember why.

They sat in silence for a moment. Then they both laughed, and Judy said, "We've just *got* to stop meeting like this." After their initial discomfort wore off, they had a surprisingly tolerable evening.

You never know what's going to happen when you agree to meet a stranger. It could be a mildly bizarre confrontation like Scott and Judy's, or it could be more commonly distressing, like, for instance, that you totally despise each other at first sight. The man may very well turn out to be dull as dishwater, grotesquely ugly, looking for something kinky, married, or even someone you already know (one woman found out from "personals experience" that her co-worker's husband was looking for a little extra fun). While it's great to be pro-active about your dating life, it can be downright terrifying to actually come face to face with someone you found through an advertisement.

Obviously, you will want to set up a short date for your first meeting, allowing for easy termination of the date, should that be desirable. I've been told the safest and best places to meet are a museum, a coffee shop, a restaurant, or a crowded park. It is *not* acceptable to bring someone on your date with you, even if you get really, really nervous at the last minute. You may be tempted to have an undercover friend present—someone who stays in the background and pretends not to know you—but under no circumstances are you to be caught winking, waving, or sticking your tongue out at them. The same goes for preplanted "date shills." I once went on a date with a guy whose buddies just "happened" to be at the next table. I was not impressed; furthermore, I felt outnumbered and spied-upon.

Many people have a last-minute panic attack. There's a lot of buildup to this moment, and when it arrives, you may get stage fright and forget every piece of chitchat you ever knew. Here are some stock date lines for those perspiration-producing personals encounters.

DATE LINES

"It's amazing; you look just like your voice."

"How long have you been in print, personals-wise?"

"I wonder how many other people in this restaurant [coffee shop] are meeting for the first time?"

(If he picked the place) "I hate to say this but I really want to know: Do you come here often?"

"I'm really new to this; please forgive me if I don't know any of the personals etiquette."

"Well, here we are at last. Or maybe at first."

"I always feel like I'm on an interview—only I'm not quite sure what the job entails."

Chapter Five:

NONPARTY LINES:
OPENINGS FOR OTHER SITUATIONS

A woman without a man cannot meet a man, any
man, of any age, without thinking, even if it's for a
half-second, Perhaps this is the man.
—DORIS LESSING

 t was Election Day: November 5, 1996. In the el-
egant neighborhood of Gramercy Park in New
York City, an intrepid young woman named Marian (who also just happens to be my editor) entered her designated voting place. It was 6:00 P.M., prime
lever-pulling time—and very crowded. Marian was distracted
with thoughts of democracy and problems at her office;
however, she was not too distracted to notice a particularly
delicious-looking man who had signed in right before her
and was now standing in front of her in a long line for the
voting booth. He was tall, very cute, and was carrying under
his left arm *The Collected Works of Henry James, The New York
Times, The Village Voice,* and a Zippy the Pinhead comic book.
It was enough. She was smitten.

Marian wondered what she could say to him. The queue

was long, but moving steadily. She knew she had only a limited amount of time in which to give destiny a helping hand. She touched the man lightly in the general vicinity of his elbow. He turned around and looked at her quizzically. "Hello!" She smiled. "I'm Marian." She shook his hand (the one without the reading material in it) just as if they were at a fund-raiser. "As long as we're waiting in line . . . I don't know many people in my voting district."

Marian had hit on just the right note; people inside a voting poll are usually feeling patriotic, and she had presented her introduction to this man almost as if it were part of his civic duty. They had a playful conversation, voted, and went their separate ways. Since they had only exchanged first names, that—as they say—might have been that, if it weren't for the fact that the very crafty Marian had sneaked a peek over the man's shoulder when he signed in to vote. When she got home, she looked him up in the telephone book and found out that he lived across the street from her. Marian decided to take a chance and call him. Luckily, she got his machine, and left the following message: "Hi, we just met at the polls. I am *so* embarrassed to be doing this. I saw your name in the sign-in book and looked you up. I will *completely* understand if you don't call me back, but I thought you might want to meet me for coffee sometime."

It worked! The man was extremely flattered that she had tracked him down, and the two went out on several dates. Even though their first encounter did not, alas, ripen into a Relationship, it was an excellent nontraditional pickup maneuver on the part of Marian.

I have heard of people meeting their future spouses at bus stops, while standing in line, in dentists' offices, in emergency rooms, in hardware stores, in museums, and in parks.

I myself have gone out with men I've met in vintage clothing stores, pinball parlors, bookstores, on the beach, and in the laundromat. Usually these kinds of ships-passing-in-the-night meetings require more caution as well as more creativity than your average bar pickup. People who are out in public (but not at the pub) are busy, wary, and usually focussed on something else.

Ironically, the hardest men to approach can be those you already know but with whom you have established a nonromantic relationship, such as your accountant, your bank teller, your yoga instructor, your tree surgeon, your chiropractor, your local donut seller—or your very best friend from high school. But for sheer excitement and romance, there is nothing like the street pickup.

The Bold Line: Street Pickups

One sunny day I was standing on a street corner on the Upper West Side in Manhattan, waiting for a friend. She was late. I don't like standing alone on the street in this particular neighborhood because there are a lot of homeless people who approach you, especially if you are standing still. As if in answer to my fear, a bedraggled-looking inebriated man came weaving up to me.

"Hey, wanna . . . cmrelll . . . w'me?"

"No, thank you," I replied firmly. (Not that I understood him.) I turned away, hoping he would get the message. Unfortunately, his antenna for receiving such messages was long since broken. He became more insistent.

"Hey! Gimmmmeee a dollar, y'beautiful wmshshsss . . ."

It was becoming clear to me I wasn't going to get him to go away. Like most people, I give away spare change when I can, but this person seemed dangerous; there was something decidedly menacing about him. I tried saying sharply, *"No!"* but he just kept coming closer and getting louder. I looked around for an escape, wondering if I was going to have to give up waiting for my friend to avoid this person.

Suddenly, another man, who was walking along the sidewalk about ten yards away, waved gaily at me and ran up beside us. The newcomer was nice-looking, well-dressed, and had a big, welcoming smile on his face.

"Hi!" he said, shaking my hand vigorously. "I am so sorry I'm late! Have you been waiting long?" I felt a little dizzy; I had no idea who this man was. Was I going crazy? Then I noticed he had placed his body in between the homeless man's and mine. He leaned in close and whispered in my ear, "You looked as if you needed rescuing."

"Oh! Yes, well, it's about time you got here!" I teased back, playing along. The drunken man mumbled something and moved off down the street.

As hopelessly old-fashioned as it sounds, I was so grateful to this knight in shining Armani—and he looked so good to me compared to the guy he had helped to repel—that when he called me up that very evening (I had given him my card) I accepted a date with him without hesitation.

Most sidewalk pickups are much less dramatic than the Good Samaritan story above, and they do not necessarily take place on or in the street. They can occur on the subway, in checkout lines, post office lines, in the park, at the zoo, at a parade, at an ice-skating rink, at a gas station, in a traffic jam, inside any type of store, on a ski slope, or while swimming in a lake. One woman I know met the man who was to become her husband in a picket line. Another smashed into her future mate's car in a parking lot. Most street pickups are unplanned, although sometimes a person will find a gimmick that really works for them and they'll make a habit of it: One female "pickup artist" told me that she used to borrow an industrial-sized video camera, take it to the park, pose as a TV documentary maker, and ask good-looking men if they would be willing to go on a blind date with her as part of the project.

Since "street meets" are like snowflakes—every one is unique—it is impossible to offer lines to fit every situation. But here are some examples.

 ## DATE LINES

For standing in line

"What do you think the holdup is? Do you mind talking while we wait?"

"That is a *great* hat."

"You know, we spend an average of five years of our lives standing in line."

In movie lines

"I hope this film is worth this wait. What have you heard about it?"

"I always feel funny standing in line by myself . . . I don't suppose you're by yourself too, are you?"

In a store checkout line

"From what you're buying, it looks like you're having a party!"

"Is this the express line? Thanks. I always think that somehow if you stand in this line you are supposed to *express* yourself more."

In public elevators (as opposed to elevators in your own building)

"So what's a guy like you doing in an elevator like this?"

"I see there is no thirteenth floor here. Do you know when builders stopped including a thirteenth floor? I've always wondered."

"I dreamt about being in an elevator last night. Do you know what dreaming about elevators means?"

Waiting for subway/bus

"When I become mayor, I'm going to totally revamp the transit system."

"Have you been waiting long? People used to say men were like streetcars—if you missed one, another would come along in ten minutes. All I can say is, I sure wish *buses* were like streetcars!"

In waiting rooms

"Are you waiting for someone or are you here to see the doctor [the lawyer/the therapist] yourself."

"So, what are *you* in for?"

"Ahh . . . *People* magazine: the junk food of periodicals. It almost makes coming here worth it."

In museums/shops

"Excuse me, but I find this piece incredibly exciting; does it affect you the same way?"

"Those aren't really Georgia O'Keefe's hands in that painting, are they?"

"Pardon me, sir, but I'm in desperate need of a man (laugh). That is, I need a man's opinion on something I'm buying for a friend."

At the site of an accident, street performance, or parade

"I wonder if you can tell me what's going on; I'm sure you can see *everything,* you're so *tall.*"

THE TOURIST TRAP

This daring ploy requires a little bit of acting ability but can be fun. In the Tourist Trap, you play the part of someone who is just passing through town, even though you actually live around the corner. Select your victim (it is sometimes most effective—and also safest for you—if he is in a group), and approach him with some version of: "Excuse, me, I'm in town just for the weekend, and I was wondering if you guys knew where the best place is around here to get a hamburger [a good vegetarian meal/a great cup of coffee]."

More often than not, this approach will solicit a friendly, hopefully not too lascivious, "Well, hey, why don't you just join *us?*" And if it doesn't, you can simply say thank you and try again with someone else. Of course, if he *does* ask you to join him, you will have to lie about a lot of other things, like where you work and where you are staying and what brings you to this fair city. (You may find it gives you a thrilling sort of double-oh-seven feeling.)

One of the nicest things about the Tourist Trap is that it provides you with a built-in excuse to be at a bar or restaurant by yourself, if you happen to be a person who feels funny about things like that. Also, if you should realize at the end of the night that you were all wrong about the guy—that he's not your type after all—you don't have to worry about his calling you. You can throw him back into the sea of men with a casual "Look me up if you ever get to Chicago."

P.S. Don't worry about being found out. If you hit it off, he'll probably think it a compliment that you went to such lengths to meet him. (It will make a great story for your grandchildren.) And if you don't hit it off, who cares what he thinks?

Travel Lines

There is no more fertile ground for romance than the ground covered while you're traveling. Everything about travel is sexy. Strangers are seated close together, and everyone is in flux from one situation to another, whether they are just going away for the weekend or they are going to the reading of the will of their great-aunt Tillie. When you are traveling, you are usually moving at great speed. There is a vague sense of danger; anything can happen.

Nothing is more natural, therefore, than your striking up a conversation with other people you meet while traveling. If you happen to be touring a foreign country, it is almost required that you meet and talk to strangers. It is only a small step further to have your encounter be a romantic one. In fact, conversation is so easy and so natural when you are traveling, that I have only listed a few of the more unusual lines here. Try them sometime, and maybe that adventure you always say you're going to have will finally happen.

 ## DATE LINES

"Where've you been, where are you going, and what are you going to do when you get there?"

(On the plane, after the flight attendant has given his or her shpeel) "Did she just say that my seat cushion could be used as a flirtation device?"

"Oh, well, we'll always have Paris." (Note: This is not meant to be used if you actually *were* in Paris with the man. It's a *Casablanca* reference. *Casablanca* references should be made whenever possible. They breed romance.)

(While waiting for the train/plane) "The train isn't going to get here for an hour. Why don't you tell me the story of your life. I'm sure it's more interesting than anything I have to read."

"I couldn't help noticing you aren't wearing a wedding ring. Don't tell me I've actually sat down next to one of the few single men left in Northern America?"

"I'm going to the cafe car; can I bring you back anything?"

"If I fall asleep and wind up leaning against you, you *will* let me know, won't you?"

"I'm a stranger in town; can you direct me to your house?"

"I have always depended on the kindness of strangers." (Do not underestimate the power of this cliche, delivered with or without a Southern accent. It's a sexy way to say thank you to a hunky guy who's just lifted your suitcase into the luggage rack. Why is it so sexy? Because Blanche Dubois was a loose woman, so maybe you are, too.)

Crossing Lines: When You Want to Date Your Assistant, Your Accountant, or Your Acupuncturist

"I can't stand it anymore," wailed my friend Francie. "Every time he comes in to do my filing I have to stop everything I'm doing to talk to him. And I don't even know what I'm saying. He drives me wild." Francie had a bad case for Tony, the new assistant at her office. The problem: She was his boss.

It's scary to try to break through the confines of one kind of relationship to form another. First of all, there is often an unequal power structure in your current relationship, which can make asking him out awkward. Secondly, you may have mistaken his professional courtesy or eagerness to please for something more. Mixed signals are not uncommon between men and women who are together for a primarily nonsexual purpose. Does your real estate broker treat *everyone* with such loving care? Does your PR man flirt so openly with *all* his clients? You'll never know if he is interested in playing a new role in your life until you let him know you want to change the script.

One word of warning: Whatever your relationship is now, there is a good chance you are going to wreck it by bringing romance into the picture. So make sure he's not the only good masseur in town.

Disclaimer: It is unethical, even illegal, for certain boundaries to be crossed. You must be the judge as far as knowing when and if the barrier in question can be broken. I'm here only to tell you how you might proceed, once you've decided you're going to go for it.

DATE LINES

"Your workmanship is so superior. Do you mind if I ask whether you approach your recreational activities with the same fervor?"

"Oh, and one more thing: I'd like to make another appointment with you . . . for dinner, that is."

"Take a memo: Will you go out with me this Saturday? Sincerely yours, etc."

"I know it's unprofessional for a doctor to date his patient, but what's professionalism compared to romance?"

"You took the buyer to the Rainbow Room? I'm so jealous!"

Or make some "accidental" slips, just to get the flavor of sex in the air.

"Joe, if you don't get that report done I'm going to kiss you—I mean I'm going to kill you."

"Joe, can you grab that pile of papers and bring it to the bedroom—sorry! I meant the boardroom, of course. What is the matter with me!"

"Listen, Joe, for the market research thing, let's just pick some clients at condom—I mean, at random."

Shifting Gears: Asking Out Someone You Already Know as a Friend

It can sneak up on you; suddenly you find you're mooning over the guy on your softball team with whom you've been

good buddies for years. One woman I talked to said she finally just called up her friend one day and announced, "I
seem to have suddenly developed a big old crush on you."
Happily for her, the man had been feeling the same way but
hadn't known what to do about it.

If, however, you think the honest approach is too risky,
you might want to try a little trick I call "Only Make Believe" (named after the song from the Broadway musical
Showboat). What you do is ask your friend if he would mind
pretending—just for the night—to be your boyfriend. Con-
coct a good reason for needing a romantically convincing
escort: your old boyfriend is going to be at the party and you
can't stand to have him see you alone, or it's your twentieth
high school reunion and you don't want your classmates to
think you couldn't snag a man. During the event, make him
go through all the motions with you: have him call you
honeybunch, put your arm around his neck, give him sensu-
ous little kisses.

Then at the end of this cozy evening, as you are having a
warm cognac together, you say something like, "It was so
much fun tonight, it felt so natural. I wonder if things had
been different whether we might have . . . been more than
friends." If he gazes at you intently and says, "Mmmmm, I
wonder," you are in good shape to proceed; if he laughs and
says, "Yeah. Too bad I'm never attracted to the nice ones like
you!" you can let the whole matter drop, ego unscathed. The
concept behind "Only Make Believe" is that sometimes, when
you get someone to play a part, he will actually start to believe it. When he sees what it could be like, it just might ap-
peal to him.

If this kind of deception is not your style, however, use a
line like one of the ones below.

DATE LINES

"Listen: Our friendship is over. (pause) Let's be more than friends."

"Do you think it would ruin our friendship if I told you I sometimes think about what it would be like to kiss you?"

"I've been spending all this time looking for a sexy, smart, nice, funny man to be in love with. Then I realized the person I was imagining was a lot like . . . you."

"The funniest thing has been happening, Joe. I've been having these incredibly hot dreams about you. I know we're just friends but . . . What do you think it means?"

"I'd like to upgrade my relationship with you. What do you think it would take?"

(Or set your friend up with a blind date. What he won't know until he gets there is the blind date is you.)
"Surprise. Sally couldn't make it. I hope you're not too disappointed. I confess, I'm happy to fill in."

Chapter Six:

DATING LOGISTICS

*A kiss can be a comma, a question mark or an
exclamation point. That's basic spelling that every
woman ought to know.*
—MISTINGUETT

When two people who don't know each other
dance for the first time, there is usually a little
stumbling, some stepping on toes, a few false
starts. When two people first begin to date,
there is usually a similar sort of fumbling as they adjust their
fine-tuning to each other. The rhythm of a romance needs to
be found. From your first phone conversation to your first
kiss, there will be moments of uncertainty to be negotiated
and disasters to be deterred. A good date line or two can help
guide you through the rough dating waters; silence may be
golden, but it doesn't solve the problem of who is picking up
the check.

Facing First Phone Calls

You might think that your average intelligent woman would have no problem thinking of what to say to a man once she's finally gotten up the nerve to call him for the first time. You might think so, but you'd be wrong. I know many women who practice in the mirror, write down word for word what they want to say, or do deep-breathing exercises beforehand. We all have anxiety about the first call. It's like stepping off a cliff, and if—as the saying goes—it's not the fall that hurts you but the sudden stop at the end, the potential rejection from the man is your sudden stop.

One of my best friends uses a ruse when she wants to call a man but is not sure how her call will be received. Let's say she wants to call Mike Harrison. She dials his number, and when he answers, she says, "Hello, is Rick Harley there?" When Mike informs her that there is no Rick Harley at that number, she acts confused but pleased at hearing his voice. "Is that Mike? Mike Harrison? Oh, hi! You know what I must have done? I pulled the wrong number out of my book. Well, gosh, how are you anyway?"

This phoney phone call may be the coward's way in, but my friend claims it is 98 percent effective. If he's not interested the call will usually end without much embarrassment; if he is interested, then he doesn't care whether she was using a smoke screen or not, he's just glad she called.

Many women call their quarry when they know he'll be out, so as to avoid live confrontation. But voice mail is a first caller's worst enemy. When it's the first time you've called him—and it's you who are the one initiating things—it is almost a given that you are going to leave the most juvenile, ridiculous, humiliating message on his machine. And of course, once it's on there, you can't get it off. You sit helpless and miserable in your apartment, picturing him coming home to his answering machine. There it is, waiting for him, that maddening red light blinking away as if it were laughing at you both.

Due to the frequent occurrence of this kind of voice message debacle, most dating experts will—quite reasonably—advise you to err on the side of brevity and simplicity when you are leaving a message. I, however, have learned to face my own answering machine phobia head on, by leaving *purposefully reckless messages*. Sure, you could end up sounding like a fool, but risks are the foodstuff of life (or at least the spice); and after all, doesn't dating more or less necessitate a courageous attitude?

DATE LINES

"Hello, Bob? This is Betty. I met you at the party on Saturday? The reason I'm calling is—oh, darn! (make rustling noise) Sorry, I'm trying to put on pantyhose while I'm talking to you, believe it or not. Hold on. (more rustling noise) Anyway, I'd love to hear from you; my number is . . ."

"Hello, Bob. This is your subconscious speaking to you through your answering machine. Call Betty and ask her out—555-2435. Call Betty and ask her out—555-2435 . . ."

If, god forbid, you *should* have to talk to the real thing, you might be able to dispel some of your nervousness with one of these:

DATE LINES

"Hello, this is Mary Matthews. We met at Tom and Sue's last week? I bribed your phone number out of them. I hope you don't mind."

"My mother told me never to call boys, but she never said anything about *men.*"

"Hello. I'm calling to ask you out, and I'm really terrified to be doing it. I'd rather not say who this is until it is absolutely necessary."

"I've got some good news and some bad news. The bad news is that you have *not,* after all, won the Publishers Clearinghouse Sweepstakes. The good news is that I'm going to take you out to help you get over your disappointment."

"I just picked up the phone to call someone else but instead I dialed you. I'm not sure why. Maybe I'd like to see you."

How to Tell If You Are Really on a Date

A male friend of a friend once told me I should really meet Dino. Dino was single, straight, two years older than me, and owned a bed and breakfast in the Hamptons. Accordingly, I spoke to him on the phone and we agreed to have coffee (the nineties version of a drink.)

Now, in my universe, when someone has hooked you up with a single, straight male with no ostensible purpose but a social one, it's a date. But as is so often noted, the Male Universe and the Female Universe are not always spinning by the same laws of physics. First we did a few of his errands, like going to the bank and the post office. While we were doing errands, he answered my cheerful interrogatives about his business and living situation with monosyllables. Oddly, he was acting as if we had known each other for years and no longer felt we had to say much to each other. I wanted to be agreeable, so I was trying to follow his lead, but I was in fact getting very confused. At last we went to a cafe.

I had just begun to relax into my chair, when suddenly a woman sitting next to us interrupted what Dino was saying, and before I knew what was happening, Dino was embroiled in a lively conversation with her. The two of them spoke about this and that for twenty minutes, leaving me sitting there with a what-am-I-chopped-liver look on my face.

Finally, the other woman left. After a minute of silence (I was so deflated that I had pretty much given up trying to converse), Dino got up and put his jacket on.

"Oh, are we leaving?" I asked him, now totally convinced that he must have taken one look at me at the very beginning and decide I wasn't his type.

Then came the shocking part.

"I guess I should have picked a day when I had more time . . . do you want to get together soon and go to the movies?" I couldn't help it, really I couldn't; I simply laughed out loud. Then I said, sure, he could call me—knowing he never would. When he called me that very night I was floored.

I talked to our mutual friend the next day about my weird date with Dino and to my great astonishment, the friend said to me, "Well, it wasn't like a *date* or anything, I just thought you were both cool and you could hang out."

It is sometimes almost impossible to tell what is a date and what isn't. Some people say the encounter has to be in the evening to be a date; some people say a date must include flirting or a goodnight kiss. Others say you have to have asked the person out on the phone at least one day in advance. While I don't believe in getting hung up on labels, it can create misunderstandings when two people have different perceptions about why they are spending time together. When you get all dolled up for a hot date and the man arrives at your door with his gay lover on his arm, it can be quite a blow to your equilibrium.

Below are some sample date-detection lines. Your assessment of the whole date or nondate question should be based on the man's reaction to the line. Like most test lines, these are by no means foolproof.

 ## DATE LINES

"Are you dating much?"

ANSWER:

"Not unless you call hanging out with my girlfriend 'dating.'" Or "Yes, I had a date last night with a seriously hot babe!"

DIAGNOSIS:

These two answers indicate you are *not* on a date, or if you are, you don't want to be.

ANSWER:

"This is the first date I've been on in weeks."

DIAGNOSIS:

Bingo. Congratulations, you are on a date.

"So, what did {name of mutual friend} tell you about me, anyway?"

ANSWER:

"He told me you'd be a great gal to pal around with at flea markets."

DIAGNOSIS:

This is not a particularly good sign. He is probably interested in you only as a friend. But it has possibilities.

ANSWER:

"He told me we'd have a lot in common—he also told me you were pretty, and I must say he was right.

DIAGNOSIS:

This is an excellent date response. Full steam ahead.

ANSWER:

"Actually, he thought you'd be a really good person for me to get advice from about this woman I'm trying to romance."

DIAGNOSIS:

Oh well, you can't win them all.

"What do you like to do with your weekends?"

ANSWER:
"I like to Rollerblade; I like to go sailing or to the beach. Sometimes I like to take long walks in the park."

DIAGNOSIS:
This one scores high on the date-detection scale. This is the kind of thing a man thinks a woman wants to hear. It shows he is in shape, and that he has a sensitive side. He is trying to appear attractive to you.

ANSWER:
"Mostly I like to lie around and watch football with my buddies."

DIAGNOSIS:
This response indicates either that he is trying *not* to appear attractive to you or simply that he is a big lout. If I had to hazard a guess I would say you are not on a date with this man.

ANSWER:
"I have a friend named Jan who likes to ski and so we go to Vermont a lot."

DIAGNOSIS:
This is a cryptic reply: He might be telling you he has women friends, and you could be one of them; on the other hand, he could be letting you know he has a romance in his life. Or Jan could be a man, and then who knows what's

going on. Don't get your hopes up though, unless you are into threesomes.

One final note. Don't rule out the direct approach: "So, is this a date or what?" (If you want to soften it a bit, use a Valley Girl accent: "Is this, like, a *date* date?") It's blunt but—for better or for worse—garners fast results.

Generic Lines for Filling Awkward Silences

Awkward silences can happen because neither of you can think of anything to say, or they can happen because one of you makes a dating faux pas. One guy I know, Dennis, described a first date he had with a woman who for some reason (I think it might have been because she was drop-dead gorgeous) made him very nervous. And when he gets nervous, Dennis tends to talk a lot. On this particular occasion he began to talk at great length about how much hockey he played when he was in high school, and how much hockey he played in college; how much he likes hockey in general, and how he was so busy playing hockey in school he didn't have time to date much. Aha, Dennis thought to himself, realizing he had been going on about his hockey prowess at great length, here's a good place for a smooth segue back to my date.

"Did *you* date a lot in school?" Dennis asked her.

"Not really," she responded unsmilingly, "because where I went to school, the guys were all jocks."

FISHING LINES: A GUIDE TO INDIRECT INFO-GATHERING

I believe in honesty and straightforwardness as much as the next gal (well, maybe just a little less); on the other hand, sometimes you can really hurt yourself when you look directly into the sun. It can be off-putting to ask a man the things you really want to know, and a lot of times the things you want to know most are the things men don't want you to find out. *But ve haf vays of makink him talk.*

(Please note: Because they are meant to elicit information without actually requesting it, these fishing lines don't always work. Sometimes you have to keep casting.)

WHAT YOU WANT TO KNOW	WHAT YOU SAY TO HIM
Do you find me attractive?	"I had my hair done today and I'm not sure I like it."
Are you married?	"When you travel, where do you like to go?" (A married man will almost always reply to this with "We go to . . .")
Are you straight or gay?	"Do you remember what our waiter looked like? I want to order something else." ("I think he had dark hair" = straight; "Yes, he was blond, fabulous-looking, with a cute butt" = not straight.)
Why haven't you called?	"I found out my answering machine hasn't been working right and I've missed some calls. Did you by any chance call me?"
Dammit, why haven't you called?!	"I'm calling because I realized you must have misplaced my phone number."
Are you dating anyone else?	"I guess I'm lucky to catch a guy like you home on a Friday night."

Do you want to go out with me again?	"You know, I feel like I just closed my eyes for a *second*, and all of a sudden there are tons of movies out that I would like to see."
Do you respect women?	"What's your mother like?" ("My mom is really great" = good sign; "That woman is insane!" = bad sign.)
Do you want kids?	"Would you ever let your child watch *Barney*?" ("My kids would only be allowed to watch reruns of *Mr. Rogers*" means he wants kids; "I've never given it any thought" or "It's a moot point" means he doesn't.)
Are you afraid of commitment?	"Who do you like better from *Gilligan's Island*, Marianne or Ginger? (Marianne = commitment; Ginger = no commitment.)

There are moments in life that can seem like weeks. Whether you are enduring the stunned aftermath of your diaphragm accidentally spilling out of your pocketbook onto your salad plate or you are merely experiencing the uncomfortable date silence of the everyday kind (when both of your brains have decided to take a short sabbatical), one of these lines may bridge the gap.

DATE LINES

"It's times like these I wish I had the gift of gab."

"I'm often at a loss for words when I'm with someone as attractive as you."

(Pretend you were lost in thought for a moment.) "This morning I was reading an article about childhood memories. What's *your* favorite memory—or your most vivid one?"

(Jump-start the conversation.) "Ahh! I'm just *so* glad I'm not at work right now."

"You'll have to excuse me; I'm under so much stress sometimes my ability to talk is impaired! But I'm very happy to be here with you."

"Well. So this is dating. Is it always this quiet?"

"Excuse me. I don't know what is the matter with me. I think I have halves-heimers disease."

"Well. Let's toast: To awkward silences!"

(P.S. Never forget that the right kind of silence can be compelling and mysterious, if you can manage it without looking stiff, stuck, or unhappy. Be Greta Garbo. Be the Mona Lisa. Be Harpo Marx.)

When the Check Comes

It shouldn't be a big deal, but it often is: that uncomfortable moment when the check lands on your table and neither of you is clear what your financial arrangement is for the date. There are a lot of people who still believe the man should pay, especially on a first date, though I think this seems, at least on the surface, a patently ridiculous practice. (Of course, if the man has more money than God—and you don't—it begins to make a little more sense.) Many books will tell you the appropriate thing to do is to arrange the matter with your date beforehand, which is certainly a fine idea, and yet I hear over and over again from women how often this awkward money moment occurs.

The easiest thing to do is offer to pick up the check, if you can afford it. Erring on the side of generosity is usually safe. But there are times when your inability to pay, your unwillingness to pay, or your insecurity about paying (if, for example, you think the man really wants to pay and he'll be offended otherwise) can produce a tension over the after-dinner table, just when you should be at your most relaxed and focussing on more important things—like whether or not you are ever going to see him with his shirt off.

Whether you really want to pay, you expect him to pay, or you would prefer to split it, here are some lines to ease the transaction along.

DATE LINES

"Please, you must allow me to get this. After all, I asked *you!*"

"This always feels so awkward to me. Don't you wish there were rules about this?"

"Okay, if you insist. But it's my treat next time.

(Wave him away gallantly as you grab the check.) "I'm sorry, your money's no good here."

(With mock seriousness) "Don't you dare make a move for that check; two marksmen are instructed to shoot you if you do."

"Well, shall we call for a calculator or should we just split this down the middle?"

"A toast: To splitting the check!"

Mid-date Escapes

There is no weapon in your dating arsenal that is more important than a good mid-date escape. Without a parachute, how can you be expected to jump out of the plane again and again? Some dates are just so excruciating they simply cannot be endured. You must have emergency procedures in place if you want to preserve your mental health. In any case, you'll never be truly adventuresome in the dating world until you are confident you know where the exits are.

A relative of mine, Leigh, told me that when she was sixteen years old she was coerced into attending a country club family dance with a thirteen-year-old neighborhood boy. It didn't help a bit that Leigh was 5'6" at the time and her date was about 4'3". She was mortified—as only a sixteen-year-old can be—to be seen dancing with this boy or (worse) to have anyone think he was her boyfriend.

There she was, out on the dance floor, feeling like a piece of luggage dragged around by an unruly puppy, when suddenly she spotted the proverbial tall, handsome stranger entering the room. Catching the stranger's eye, Leigh—with inspiration born of desperation—mouthed the word *help* over her date's shoulder at him. To her delight and utter relief, the newcomer came right over and cut in! (P.S. They went out for about two months, which for many sixteen-year-olds constitutes a long-term relationship.)

Of course, there *are* more Machiavellian mid-date escape techniques. An acquaintance of mine, Jack, confessed to relying heavily on one of his own creation. Jack would habitually meet his dates at a certain upscale establishment where he knew the maître d'. One of the first things he would say to his date was that there was a terrible crisis brewing at the office, but that he had managed to slip out without anyone noticing. About ten minutes into the date, the maître d', whose name is Bill, would approach the table. "Is everything alright, sir?" he would inquire.

If Jack wanted to escape the date, he would answer, "Yes, Frederick, everything is fine." The maître d' was well rehearsed. By deliberately addressing him by the wrong name, Jack had secretly informed the maître d' that he wanted out *ASAP*. A few minutes later Bill would return, acting very apologetic.

"I'm so sorry to intrude, sir, but your office is calling." Feigning annoyance, Jack would tell his date that the office, knowing that this club was one of his favorite hangouts, must have tracked him down. Then he would make apologies and leave.

Whether your mid-date escape is completely calculated, like Jack's, or impulsive, like Leigh's, it can save your skin. A good escape hatch can mean the difference between your becoming disgusted with dating—from the fatigue or the trauma—and your feeling ready and willing to go out the very next night. In lieu of any fancy James (or Jack) Bond-like strategy, one of the lines below might suffice.

DATE LINES

"Excuse me, I have to make a phone call." (Don't come back.)

(Or, after returning from using the phone) "I just checked my messages, I'm afraid my sister is on her way to my apartment [my cousin's been taken to the emergency room/there's smoke coming out of my window]; I'll have to go. No, you stay here and finish your dinner."

"I'm going to the women's room." (Don't come back.)

(Or, after returning from the women's room) "I'm sorry . . . I have to leave *immediately;* it's a female thing."

"Oh, no! I just remembered I left my stove on!"

"I hate to do this to you, but I'm getting a migraine and in about twenty minutes I won't be able to see straight . . . No, that's alright, I'll take a cab [walk—the air will do me good]."

"I really should have called earlier and reschedule this date. It turns out I have a breakfast meeting at 6:00 A.M. and I'm not fully prepared for it."

Act as if you've suddenly thought of something. Rifle frantically through scraps of paper in your purse. Then yell, "OH MY GOD—I THINK I WON LOTTO!" and run out of the room.

"Uh-oh. I'm getting that feeling . . . I think I'm having one of my spells . . ." (Then stare off into space, glassy-eyed.)

The First Kiss (Ducking or Expediting)

Let's hope it's truly magical. You've had a fabulous first date, you are mutually attracted to each other, the stars are out. Your eyes meet. You are drawn together electromagnetically until your lips . . . touch.

Sometimes the first kiss with a new man is like this, more often it's not. You may be nervously obsessing about seemingly trivial things ("Is my purse going to be in the way? Are too many people watching?" Or even, "Do I have garlic breath?"), but more frequently your brain is in a frenzy of wondering if he *wants* to kiss you, if he's *going* to kiss you, and whether or not *you* want to kiss him. Funnily enough, as many stories as I have heard of people being shocked at receiving an unexpected kiss, I have heard just as many from women who were surprised that a kiss never happened. It's obvious that pre-kiss communication is not always perfect. One friend reminisced wincingly about her first kiss with an old boyfriend; unbeknownst to him, she had had way too much to drink. When he leaned in at the strategic moment, she also leaned—over his lap to throw up. ("How romantic," was his memorable comment.)

I'll never forget my own very *first* first kiss. With the boy's father waiting in the car, we walked up the steps of my brightly lit front porch, both as uptight as only twelve-year-olds on their first date can be. When we got to the very top step, the porch light suddenly went out, as if on cue. My mother had been watching from the window and—in a Bizarro World reversal of typical parental instinct—wanted me to have some privacy for my very first romantic moment. Unfortunately, the unexpected eeriness of the light suddenly going off had a countereffect on my date. He gave me a paranoid peck (on the lips, at least!) and then ran down the steps as if the porch was on fire.

In general, no matter who is the sexual aggressor afterwards, men like to initiate the very first kiss. But this is by no means a hard and fast rule. If the man isn't used to thinking of you "that way," or is very shy, you might want to do what my female friends call "pounce." The first, or ice-breaking kiss, is often a quick kiss. Some people like to get the kiss out of the way, and so kiss when they begin their date—although most do tend to use a kiss to punctuate the end of the date. Never forget your nonverbal option for helping to manifest a kiss: the stolen kiss, in which you pretend to kiss his cheek, then accidentally stumble into his lips. But you might also try one of these lines for expediting the goodnight kiss.

DATE LINES (EXPEDITING)

"Okay, let's get this kissing thing over with."

"Are you going to kiss *me* goodnight, or am I going to kiss *you* goodnight?"

"If you're thinking about kissing me then I have to tell you I like the way you think."

"If you want to kiss me, please kiss me on the lips, which is what God made them for."

"Isn't it about time we kissed?"

(After agreeing about something, such as where to go for coffee) "Great. Let's seal it with a kiss."

(You can always try a little Italian.) "Bacciami!" (Kiss me.)

If somehow your stay-away-from-me signals are misinterpreted as take-me-you-fool vibes, it is usually a fairly simple matter to dodge the goodnight kiss. All you have to do is get out of the way (it helps to keep moving) or maneuver your body so that the attempted kiss detonates harmlessly on the top of your hat or your shoulder. However, there are some men who for one reason or another won't sense—or don't respect—your antikiss attitude. I've interviewed some women who told me they spent the last half of the evening worrying about how to avert the kiss without incurring too much embarrassment. For avoiding facial *and* body contact, use the Shake and Break (stick out your hand to shake his good night); for ducking just the kiss, try the Hug-off (give him a very quick platonic hug and then back away fast). There are also some old-fashioned methods that still work fairly well: Chew a huge wad of gum, or light a big, cheap cigar just before parting. Or try:

 ## DATE LINES (DUCKING)

(Sniffling a little) "God, my sinuses are killing me; I hope I'm not getting a virus."

"Darn! I think I'm getting a vicious cold sore."

(Gaily) "Sorry, but I never kiss anyone on Thursdays."

"If you're going to kiss me I think you should know that anyone who kisses me has to come to Sunday dinner and meet my four brothers."

(Dramatically, with your hand up in front of your face, palm outward or over his mouth) "No . . . don't . . . I want to remember our evening just as it was . . . Farewell! (While he is looking at you as if you're crazy, you will hopefully have time to slip inside your house or into a taxi.)

And When He Wants to Come in for a "Nightcap:"

"A nightcap? Never wear 'em."

"I *would* ask you in but my Doberman doesn't like strangers."

"No, I really *can't* ask you in, my place is a pigsty right now . . . No, believe it or not my phone is out of order, but there's one down on the corner . . . Yes, there's a rest room there too . . . Oh, was that your head the door smashed against? I *am* sorry—g'night!"

Chapter Seven:

HANDLING REJECTION (OR, EVERY CLOUD HAS A SILVER DATE LINE)

Time wounds all heels.
—JANE ACE

The biggest hazard in dating is the potential of rejection. Now, I realize that men have to face rejection from women too; however, from the stories I've heard, I am forced to conclude that women bear the biggest brunt of the brushing off—in the *quality* of the brush-off, not the quantity. I don't know whether or not men have a natural tendency to be insensitive to other people's feelings (I'll leave that for the psychologists and biologists to squabble about). All I know is that a large number of them seem to choose to dump the women they date by telling them they aren't good-looking enough, sexy enough, or smart enough. A lot of men flirt with other women while on dates. Some deliberately leave other women's clothes lying around their apartments; some say things like, "You're not the woman I thought you were" (as if somehow the women have tricked them). Many guys ignore their dates, or simply vanish, like burglars in the night, without a word of explanation.

Admittedly, we are not talking about serious heartbreak here; in the dating stage the most you suffer is ego bruising. But whenever I hear a particularly callous man-rejecting-woman story, it makes me wonder if, in fact, men aren't aliens. I mean this literally. I know the author of *Men Are from Mars, Women Are from Venus* meant it as a metaphor, but the more I think about it the more convinced I am that when the Earth was made, God took one species from one part of the galaxy and another species from another part and flung them down in the foliage together in some sort of hideous social experiment. Anyway, it may help to keep this theory in mind the next time the guy you've been dating for a month tells you he's dumping you for a twenty-year-old named Barb because she has better hair and longer nails than you. Part of you will be able to step back and think, "Men: What an odd and fascinating species."

Then again, after you've taken a second to see the little darling in this anthropological light, it's also pretty good for your self-esteem if you can zing the bastard with a "barb" of your own.

When He Hasn't Called

It's happened to you again. You had a nice evening with a man. You laughed, you ate, you went to the movies. He said repeatedly how much he wanted to take you to the races at Saratoga and other places you've never been. He asked you when you got up in the morning so he could call you. You kissed goodnight under a big tree, which you know you'll never look at the same again. You go to sleep that night thinking of him.

And then, the next day . . . nothing. You check your phone throughout the day to make sure it's working. (It is.) You tell yourself, it's just that man time–woman time thing. He'll call in a day or so. You hitch up your pants and get back to the details of your life, forcing yourself not to think about him more than once an hour.

A week or two later you've stopped trying to figure out why he hasn't called. Now you're trying to figure out why you don't give up and move to an ashram in Bali. In other words, you're really pissed, and you feel that—for the sake of womankind, mind you, not for any petty emotional reason like your feelings being hurt—if you see him you're going to let him have it. (And if you don't see him you're going to *call* him and let him have it.)

DATE LINES

"What a surprise to see you—and looking so well, too. When I didn't hear from you, I was sure something must have happened to you."

"If men are from Mars, they must not have phones there."

"Don't tell me. Your cat ate my number."

"Oh, hi! Listen, I'm *SO* sorry if you've been trying to call; I had my number changed."

"Well, hello there. I thought you were dead. Wishful thinking, I guess."

"Oh, hi! I am so embarrassed—I had *such* a good time the other night, but I cannot for the *life* of me remember your name."

When He Ignores You

It was one of those dreadful blind date experiences you wish you could electronically delete from your memory. His name was Harry something. He was blond, handsome, and super cool; he had Andover and Harvard and summers in Europe written all over him. I, on the other hand, was a pseudohippie at the time, sporting long frizzy hair and vintage clothes. I could tell from the way he glanced at me when he picked me up (in his cream-colored convertible) that he was disappointed, though I tried to tell myself things would improve as he got to know me. (Hah!)

He drove me to a bar and placed me with great solicitude on a particular barstool. I was tickled to be the object of such attentiveness until I realized that he only wanted to make sure he was facing the TV, through which was blaring (naturally) a football game. I became The Invisible Woman. Every now and then his eyes would flicker blankly back to me, but for the most part he remained engrossed in the game. I could have taken my clothes off and he wouldn't have noticed.

I don't remember exactly what I said or did. I think I

drank a little too much and made a huge effort to be entertaining. Unfortunately, my date had checked out as soon as he met me, so there was no one to entertain.

Here's the kind of thing I *should* have said, and more important, what *you* should say if you are ever confronted by this type of rude neglect. (Please note: The first three lines are designed specifically for when you have been deemed Less Interesting Than Television; the rest are for other kinds of ignoring—like when your date talks to someone else all night, or simply stares off into space.)

DATE LINES

"You know, I just *love* the way your eyes look with the TV reflected in them."

"Have you ever considered getting one of those Sony Watchmans?"

(As you are getting up to leave) "Why don't you call me when the football season is over. (Pause.) On second thought, don't."

"Don't you know there is a law in this state that says you are required to spend at least thirty minutes with the person you went out with? Are you trying to get arrested?"

"It's obvious that you are either bored or that something is bothering you. In either case perhaps it might be better if we cut this date short."

"Men are from Mars, and it doesn't matter where women are from because you're not listening anyway."

(Softly) "Excuse me, Joe. I don't mean to interrupt your conversation with your friends, but when you have some time I really want to talk to you about oral sex."

And for those especially delightful occasions when your date hasn't been near you all night and has left you standing or sitting alone:

"Excuse me? Hi! I'm Susan Jones. And you are . . . ? Oh, of course—my *date!* It's been so long, I'd forgotten."

"Hello? Remember me? (Smile warmly.) Well, take a real good look at this face, darlin', because you won't be seeing it again." (Exit.)

When He Dodges Your Forward Pass

This won't happen often. Men are not designed to spurn the physical advances of women. That's why when you *do* decide to plant one on him, and he tenses up (not in a good way) or turns away in disgust, it is your worst nightmare come to life. Death by mortification.

It's hard enough for a woman to overcome the several centuries of social conditioning she needs to in order to make the pass, but when that pass is subsequently rebuffed, she can often wish she had never been born. And if the object of her unwanted desire happens to be her boss, or her best friend's roommate, then she'll wish *he'd* never been born. It is for these types of moments that the single girl needs a good, strong survival line to grab onto, to keep her from being destroyed by embarrassment.

DATE LINES

"I'll give you twenty dollars to pretend that never happened."

"I'll give you fifty dollars to kill me right now."

"I don't know what is the matter with me. This new allergy medication is really affecting me weirdly."

"Wow. Are you wearing a new cologne?"

"I have to apologize. I just did that on a dare. Somebody bet me I wouldn't. Forgive me?"

"Sorry, I guess my personal radar detector is on the blink!"

(Ironically) "Well, *that* certainly went well."

Battle Lines: When Your Date Insults You

This is a true story. Only the names have been changed to protect the humiliated. One spring day Sarah decided to answer a personal ad, through which she made the acquaintance of an interesting-sounding man named Charles. Sarah and Charles corresponded by mail, and at Charles' suggestion, exchanged photographs of each other. Finally, they made a date. They agreed that Charles would come to Sarah's house to pick her up.

Sarah was a little nervous when she opened the door. This was the first time in a couple of years that she had made a date with a stranger.

According to Sarah, the very first thing the man said to her when she opened the door was, "What? *You're kidding!*"

She was flabbergasted. "What do you mean?" she asked, confused and alarmed.

"You don't look anything like your picture! What a gyp." Sarah was speechless. (The picture she had sent, Sarah swore to me, had been a recent one.) Her face flushed, and her jaw dropped open and stayed there. Charles brushed past her into her apartment. "I don't see this as working out. You're not as attractive as I thought you were."

Sarah was still trying to fathom what was happening, but words would not come.

"Can I use your phone?" Automatically, she motioned him to the one in the kitchen. Unbelievably, the man whipped out a typed list of names and numbers and proceeded to call another woman for a date!

When he finished, he said to Sarah, "Thanks. At least now the evening won't be totally wasted." And with a hasty "Sorry it didn't work out" over his shoulder, he left.

If this account was not exaggerated, this man was insulting to such an extreme level that it borders on the psychotic. But there are a lot of men who (especially when they are using the personals) feel completely justified in being outraged if you don't measure up to their expectations—especially physical ones.

I have also heard or read about men insulting their date's attire, beliefs, food selection, laugh, diction, or career. Some of the women I talked to had been called gold diggers, bimbos, ball-busters, and femi-nazis on dates. You never know when you might end up sitting across the table from someone who is going to make unpleasant comments to you about PMS, hormones, or even "lady drivers."

Occasionally you will be insulted on the phone before you actually go out on the date, which is painful but much easier to deal with than an in-person affront. One woman I know was interviewing a potential date on the phone. They talked for about an hour. They laughed, they had a great deal in common; she felt comfortable with him. Then, just as they were about to make a date, he paused.

"Ah, one more thing. Can you tell me more about what you look like?" (Her ad had only designated hair and eye color.)

"Well, what do you want to know?" the woman asked him.

"Your weight . . . Tell me how much you weigh." The woman, like most, was not used to giving out this information, so she demurred. He asked her dress size. Finally, embarrassed, she said, "Fourteen, I guess."

There was a silence. And then he said, "I'm afraid I have an issue with that." (An *issue?*)

The worst thing about this interaction, the woman told me, was that she automatically responded by saying, "I'm sorry." What she should have said was, "Don't tell me. I bet I'm just too much woman for you." Or, "Well, it's just as well, because I have an issue with assholes." (Click.)

One important thing to remember before using one of the lines below: If you *are* out with Mr. Rude and Obnoxious, you may just make him behave worse by trading insults with him. It's not exactly the high road. However, when you feel abused enough that you've got to say *something,* and you would like it to be more than *"Oh, yeah?"* then one of these comebacks could be your ticket to self-respect. (Note: To avoid inciting him to greater piggishness and getting into a screaming match, deliver the line right before you are about to hang up, drive away, or slam the door in his face. You have to make sure you are going to have the last word.)

DATE LINES

"Listen: Just because you picked me up doesn't mean you can put me down."

"Have you given any serious thought to therapy?"

"Wow. If you're the man of my dreams I sure want to wake up."

"You know, women only smile at you because they are trying hard not to laugh."

"Is this a date or open heart surgery?"

"Is this a date or Chinese water torture?"

"I think the rudeness police have a warrant out for your arrest."

Or Use Sarcasm:

"Wow. Could you be a *little* more hostile?"

"Well, well. Mr. Congeniality."

"I bet you were a real charmer in high school."

"You know, when you say things like that, I just go all warm and fuzzy inside!"

(See also Killer Kiss-Offs, page 120.)

Upon Being Officially Dumped

Helen told me a great breakup story. He took her out for her birthday. It was their fifth or sixth date. They went to a great, expensive restaurant, then out dancing, then back to her place. Both slightly tipsy, they started fooling around. It had been such a perfect night, and Helen was so enamored of this man, that they ended up in her bedroom.

HOW TO RECOGNIZE REJECTION
FROM THE MALE SPECIES

Most men are basically chicken when it comes to telling you they don't want to continue dating you. You sometimes have to listen through a special man filter. When you hear any of the following phrases from a man, you may be receiving your walking papers. (Note: Some of these are almost impossible to distinguish from positive signals; that's just how this lovable species works.)

"I'll call you."

"I think you are a really interesting person."

"I just want you to know I care a lot about you."

"You deserve someone who is as nice as you."

P.S. If in a written communique a man refers to your "relationship" (in quotes), better say sayonara, señore.

The next morning Helen, glowing, cooked him breakfast. It was over the second cup of coffee that the bomb fell.

"I need to tell you something," he said. This is never a good sentence to hear from a man, especially first thing in the morning, but Helen was obliviously enjoying her new romance.

"What?" she asked him, stuffing the last bite of muffin into her mouth.

"I can't see you anymore."

Helen choked on the muffin. After her windpipe was clear, she looked at him incredulously. "What are you talking about . . . what about last night, for god's sake?"

He looked at her innocently and shrugged. "Well, it was your birthday. I didn't want to ruin the evening, so I thought I'd wait until today."

I don't mean to imply that there aren't plenty of men who will let you down in a gentlemanly, caring way. Indeed, most of the time when a guy tells you he doesn't want to see you anymore, he uses one of the accepted breakup stand-bys—phrases that have been used by men and women for decades, such as "I really like you, but just as a friend." But no matter how the jilting is done, you are going to want to have a good comeback ready, so you don't end up just sitting there with scrambled egg on your face and tears in your eyes.

(Note: I have tried to offer a wide range of responses to correspond to the many different ways you can be dumped or declined, including when you ask a man out for the first time and he turns you down.)

DATE LINES

"It's okay. I never really thought you were Mr. Right, you were just Mr. Right Now."

"Wow. I never expected to get the brush-off from a man with so little hair."

"I've heard about men like you, who have a problem with Premature Rejection."

"Don't worry about me. To tell you the truth, I probably won't even remember your name in a month or so."

If he says, "I still want to be friends" or "I like you, but only as a friend:"

(Smiling) "Well, as your friend, I must tell you you're making a big mistake."

(Or, make a toast.) "Well, here's to the both of us having better luck elsewhere!"

Chapter Eight:

REJECTING HIM (PHONE, FAX, OR FACE TO FACE)

A man on a date wonders if he'll get lucky. The woman already knows.
—MONICA PIPER

hat if the high-heel is on the other foot, and you find yourself in the position of being the one dashing *his* romantic aspirations? Maybe he's a jerk, maybe he's just not your type, or maybe you've suddenly decided to devote your life to the Sisterhood for Sainted Celibacy. Whatever your reasons for spurning his advances, it can be as painful to inflict the wound as it is to receive it. It is essential for your own psychological health and dating karma that you find the appropriate manner in which to reject him.

The Polite But Final Date Exit Line

I had had one of those days that give people nervous breakdowns, and I couldn't believe that I had scheduled a blind date at the end of it. I was meeting him at a little pasta place downtown. In keeping with the timbre of the day, I was twenty minutes late. The waitress ushered me to a table where my date was sitting, already eating his dinner. He was extremely skinny and had an odd, square-ish haircut. He was also obviously annoyed that I was late. At least, I thought to myself, I won't have to worry about his asking me out again. (Wrong.)

Throughout dinner, he talked mostly about his ex-wife and his bank account. He insisted on going to an after-dinner place for coffee, over which we talked more about his ex-wife, and about the various women he had been out with since his divorce. (A tip to any men who may be reading this: On a first date, women do not really love to talk about other women you've been involved with.)

At long last we paid the check and got into a cab. I was so glad to be finally putting this evening out of its misery, I didn't pay much attention to the fact that this guy was walking me to my door. In fact, so tired and stressed out was I that without thinking about what I was doing, I kissed him goodnight on the cheek, smiled, and said, "Well, I'll see ya soon."

"Great," he said. "I'll call you tomorrow."

It wasn't until I had gotten inside my apartment that I fully realized what I had done: I had unintentionally given this man a signal that I was looking forward to seeing him again. That meant I was going to have to deal with turning him down over the phone later when he called to ask me out.

It makes life much easier for everyone if you can manage to gently give the guy the thumbs-down sign at the end of the date. It has to be subtle; you certainly don't want to embarrass a nice guy by saying, "Well, thanks for dinner, but I don't find you attractive or interesting, and I'm never going out with you again." The following lines are meant to *insinuate* finality, not to pronounce it. (Sometimes the message will be lost on a man, and then you will have to deal with him later anyway.) And if he *still* asks, "Can I call you?" never say "I'd rather you didn't." Unless he has done something ratty enough to deserve a killer kiss-off, reply with a casual but unenthused "Sure." When and if he calls, you can then tell him you are entering your busy season, that your old boyfriend has come back from China, or that you liked him a lot but have just met someone you like a little more.

DATE LINES

"It was so nice to meet you."

"Take care, now."

"See y'around."

"Well, it's certainly been an eventful evening."

"I am glad we got to do this—especially as my schedule is so crazed these days."

"Good-bye, and good luck."

"Ciao."

"Bye! Have a great summer [winter/spring/fall]!"

Kind Kiss-offs

Mary confessed to me that deep down she knew she didn't re-ally like the guy. She had gone out with him only because she hadn't been on a date in a while. He was pleasant enough, but she found him, quite frankly, boring. She was more or less just going through the motions. At the end of the night, when her date suddenly said without warning, "Is this the point where I kiss you goodnight?" Mary reacted without thinking and yelped a loud *"No!"*

Another woman, Deb, told a similar story about a man she went out with who, for various reasons, she found disap-pointing (For one thing, he didn't have one fork, knife, or plate in his kitchen). When this man asked Deb if he could see her again, she couldn't think of anything to say, and in an attempt to stall, uttered a school-marmish "We'll see."

It may save you (and him) from the unpleasantness of such awkward moments if you have a few considerate kiss-off lines committed to memory.

DATE LINES

"I enjoyed spending this time with you, but I don't really think we're a good match."

"I wish I was sane enough to be attracted to someone as healthy as you, but I guess it's back to my therapist."

"I thought I was ready to meet someone new, but I guess I'm not."

"I don't want to hand you some line; the truth is you're just not my type—and don't ask what my type is because I haven't met it yet!"

Using flattery is an obvious and yet effective device for softening the blow-off

"We don't have enough in common to go out, but . . .

. . . you are the best dancer I ever met."

. . . you made me feel like a woman again."

. . . you made me laugh so hard I feel weak."

Or: "You're too . . .

. . . good-looking for me."

. . . classy for me."

. . . much of a high achiever."

Killer Kiss-offs

These conversational kicks to the head are reserved for guys who are just really asking for it. For example:

Paulo was from Brazil and very intense. We went on three dates, at the end of which he appeared to be completely smitten by me. I harbored vague hopes that maybe I would catch up to him. (I mean, how often does a man rave about your beauty?) Anyway, what with my overly optimistic attitude and a few cultural differences, somehow old Paulo got the wrong idea.

He went away on a trip to Brazil; he was very romantic about how much he was going to miss me (I *am* a sucker for accents). He told me how much he was looking forward to seeing me when he got back.

Several weeks went by, and I noticed I was receiving a lot of mail from this guy, considering I had only seen him a few times. But I was busy, and I didn't think about it too much. One day, the phone rang and it was Paulo. I was glad to hear from him. We chatted for a few minutes and then he said he wanted to see me—*immediately.* I told him I couldn't that night, as I had made plans to go with a friend to a concert.

"Cancel it," he said darkly. I refused. Sullenly, he said okay, that we would see each other the next night. Something in his voice began to make me nervous.

"Oh, darn, I *am* sorry, Paulo, tomorrow's my poker night."

(This was true.) Silence. A kind of scary silence. I added quickly, "But I'd love to see you the next night. . . . Okay?"

Suddenly I was in the middle of the kind of scene you love to see in the movies, but when it's happening to you it's a real drag. There were threats and accusations from Paulo. He was extremely angry. He accused me of not being interested in him, of toying with him, of lying to him, of being a flirt. I had to keep reminding myself I had only been out with him three times; from the way he was acting, we were in a serious relationship. And not a modern relationship, at that—he declared that it was going to be my "busy social life," or him. I was incredulous.

"Paulo, are you giving me an ultimatum?" Even my dialogue was sounding melodramatic now.

"You—you—cancel your poker game or we're through!"

My choice was clear. "Well, I guess we're through." There was another moment of that same scary silence. Then he said, icily: "You will *never* find a man. You are a *fool* to refuse me." For once I was on my toes.

"On the contrary," I said, "I would be a fool *not* to refuse you."

Handle the following killer kiss-offs with care. They can be harmful and are not to be doled out indiscriminately; they are only for times when it's either you or him.

 ## DATE LINES

"Why don't you go torture some other woman?"

"Don't look now, but I think there is a spaceship out there waiting to take you to another dimension."

"Men like you should have warning labels on them."

(Sweetly) "Has anyone ever told you you're really wonderful? No? Then where did you get the idea?"

"I can't possibly go out with someone as ignorant as you; I bet you think trains whistle at crossings to keep their courage up."

"I have heard that men are from Mars, so why don't you take a flying leap?"

"I'd like to give you a piece of my mind but I don't think you'd know what to do with it."

"I don't have time to talk about this right now. Can't it wait until we're dead?"

"I hope we'll always be friends . . . long-distance friends."

You: "Are you free Saturday?"
Him: "Yes, I am."
You: "Good. That's the night the compulsive liars [sex addicts/sexist pigs] recovery group meets. Have a good time."

"Carbolic acid to you, darling—that's good-bye in any language."

By fax or E-mail

To: Him
From: You
Regarding: Possibility of dating
This is to inform you that I am going to be tied up in a meeting . . . for the rest of the year.
Sincerely yours,

———

Creative Kiss-offs

I have often been accused of being a proponent of lying. In fact, one man I met in San Francisco told me he had no use for my books, because my conversational strategies for navigating situations were based on telling fibs; he explained that he was "an authentic." (I couldn't help wondering how many women he had "authentic-ed" into tears by telling them that in all honesty he found them unattractive—or unenlightened.)

While it is true that in an ideal world we would be able to tell people hard truths in an atmosphere of such love and self-acceptance that no pain would result, this is simply not possible in today's world. Social lying is still a part of what makes us civilized, and part of what makes us considerate adults. It's all very well to unleash our inner children (or our inner tongues) but there are some situations that call for a little sensitivity—and, yes, a few untruths.

Creative kiss-offs are particularly useful for turning a guy down when he asks you out for the first time, when you would like to spare his feelings—and still be certain he goes away. (Caution: Mendacity does carry its own risks; you do have to remember what you said. Try either to tell a lie that is only an exaggeration of the truth, or to tell the same lie to everyone so you won't forget it.)

DATE LINES

Creative Kiss-off #1: "It's not you, it's me."

This classic kiss-off has been the subject of many jokes in the singles culture (for example, on *Seinfeld*: "She used the it's-not-you-it's-me routine on *you?* But that's *your* routine!"). The fact is, this "routine" works. The following creative kiss-offs are variations on "It's not you, it's me." The real key to the it's-not-you-it's-me kiss-off is what comes after.

"It's not you, it's me . . .

. . . I am afraid of men."

. . . I don't know what I want."

. . . I can't make a commitment."

. . . I'm in love with someone else."

"I'm not comfortable with men who are as powerful as you are . . . it's a father thing."

"The truth is, I've had so many responses to my ad that I'm totally overwhelmed at the moment. I'll take your number . . ."

"I'm getting over a bad relationship and I'm just not ready to date anyone. If I were, it would be you."

"I shouldn't have come out at all tonight; I just got back together with my boyfriend. I didn't know it was going to happen when I made the date with you."

"I'm about to go on jury duty, and I think we might be sequestered. For a long time."

"I'm gay. But if I weren't . . ."

Creative Kiss-off #2: The Hit Man

In the Hit Man Kiss-off, you get someone else to do your dirty work. (Note: Someone's got to be really bugging you for you to go as far as the Hit Man.)

"Hello, John? You don't know me, but Sheila asked me to call you. I don't know anything about it, but she told me to tell you she can't see you again."

"Hello, is this John Jacobs? This is Sheila Simmons' assistant calling. Yes—Ms. Simmons asked me to call you and say that her schedule is going to be very tight for the next couple of months."

"Hello, John Jacobs? This is Sheila Simmons' mother. Sheila got married yesterday."

Creative Kiss-off #3: The Turn-off

This is when you intentionally become unappealing to the man so that he will no longer be interested in pursuing you. Men use this passive-aggressive technique all the time; it's a little harder for women to pull off, as we are trained from birth to try to please people. This is another reason to try using this kiss-off; consider it assertiveness training. (Be sure to tailor this kiss-off to the man in question; one man's Phyllis Diller is another man's Madonna.)

(Giggling) "I can't believe how many men I've dated and how I can't remember any of their names."

"I just want you to know that I am not going to have sex again until I get married."

"Would you like to take me shopping?"

"I've rented the entire series of *Little House on the Prairie* and I want you to watch it with me this weekend."

"I'd *love* to go out with you again; all you have to do is sign this pre-nuptial agreement I had drawn up."

Chapter Nine:

DATES FROM HELL: TRULY BIZARRE DATES AND OTHER EMERGENCY SITUATIONS

Things are always darkest just before they go pitch black.
—KELLY ROBINSON

ates are a little like laboratory experiments: You mix a bunch of elements together under extremely combustible conditions, and every once in a while there is going to be a major disaster. Usually it doesn't kill you but it always scares the hell out of you. Ideally, you will learn from each experiment—to watch for warning signs, or to refrain from combining those particular elements in the beaker again. But sometimes, no matter what precautions you take, accidents cannot be avoided.

Physical Mishaps

We've all had the more benign kind of physical mishap on dates: the run in a stocking, the button coming off a blouse, a broken heel, a ripped seam, a wine or food spill. Almost as common (especially in the beginning of a girl's dating career) are date accidents of a vehicular type—the car goes up on a curb or hits a tree because you can't stop staring at him; a policeman interrupts a smooching session to announce you are illegally parked. Or of a corporeal type—you discover you have an ugly cold sore, or an unsightly hang nail.

Then there's the other type of physical mishap, the kind my friend Trudy has. Trudy, who is a really wonderful actress and as graceful as a gazelle on the stage, is pathologically accident prone whenever she is on a date. One time she and a date went Rollerblading together. It was only their second date. Not surprisingly, Trudy lost control going down a hill and, also not surprisingly, broke her ankle. She and her date ended up in the emergency room, along with Trudy's overprotective father and brother. They proceeded to put the now sheepish date through the ringer, making him feel he was to blame for the accident.

Trudy had no choice but to say good-bye to her date at the hospital exit. Her foot was bandaged up to the knee, and her father was glaring at them from across the room. She managed an apologetic smile and tried to make a joke. "Well, thanks for a lovely day . . . I never thought I would fall for you so hard."

The date smiled weakly. "And I never thought I could make your family hate me this fast!"

DATE LINES

"Are we having fun yet?"

"The god of Dating is not smiling on us [on me]."

"I *hate* when that happens."

"Maybe we're both having a really bad dream."

"So is this your idea of a perfect date, or what?"

"What *else* could go wrong?"

(If you've "tossed your cookies" on a date) "Hold on a minute, I think my head's about to spin around now."

For spills and drippings

"I'm just trying to get you to notice my figure by dropping things all over it."

"By the way, did I tell you I was brought up in a barn?"

For falling buttons and other clothing catastrophes

"My heart's beating so fast I think it made my button pop off."

"I guess I'm so excited to be out with you my clothes are falling off!"

Kinky Stuff

It doesn't only happen in bad B movies. Every once in a while even the most normal woman comes up against something that lies squarely in the realm of the kinky. I have heard many true stories from average, everyday, looking-for-Mister-Right women who had dates who wanted them to dress up as French maids, beat them with paddles, be tied up, stepped on, or worse.

Most of the time when you are faced with this sort of wackiness, the best thing to do is make a polite and hasty retreat. However, you may occasionally feel compelled to use one of the comments below, if only to help dispel your own queasiness.

DATE LINES

"Wow—does your mother know about this?"

"Can I take a rain check on that?"

"You're not exactly Richie Cunningham, are you."

"I'm afraid I'm not into physical pain . . . just deep psychological and spiritual pain."

"Toto, I don't think we're in Kansas anymore."

Gender Revelations

Jim was a really nice guy. I met him at a Gloria Steinem lecture in the East Village. He was certainly not perfect. He was balding, round-shouldered, and in general had a somewhat unkempt appearance. He didn't have much of a career, and even less money. But—hallelujah—he was single, and he really seemed to like me. He also had a sexy, deep, gravelly voice; twinkly eyes; and a thick, bushy red beard I found appealing. He was intelligent and educated, to boot.

I was thrilled when he started asking me out. We had fun, casual dates just like the ones modern single people are supposed to have; we were getting to know each other well before getting physical. Jim was—miracle of miracles—a true feminist, and sensitive while somehow managing to be macho. After all the trouble with men I had had over the years, I couldn't believe my luck in finding him. (DANGER, WILL ROBINSON.)

I started getting a little anxious after we had been seeing each other for a month, and I realized the most we had done was hug goodnight. It was obvious he was attracted to me (unless my radar was totally on the blink due to atrophied muscles). My friends were all telling me to pounce, but I'm just not much of a pouncer.

One night we went out to dinner. We had a couple of drinks and before I knew it, we were discussing our previous relationships, which as anyone knows is almost always a precursor to romance. (He said his previous girlfriend and he were still friends.) We flirted, we promised things with our eyes. We paid the check.

But outside the restaurant, he suddenly became extremely nervous. "I . . . I have something I need to tell you." Uh-oh, I thought. My apartment was nearby, so we went there to talk. As we arranged ourselves on the sofa and I noticed his hands were actually shaking, my mind perused a panorama of possibilities, from herpes to bigamy. Jim hemmed and hawed, and finally intimated that the problem had something to do with a certain joke I had made the day before.

I tried to think back, stymied, until I remembered vaguely an offhanded comment I had made—during a conversation about health insurance and Hillary Clinton—about sex change operations. "Okay," I kidded. "I know you're *not* trying to tell me you're going to become a woman."

He shook his head. *"No,"* he said, sounding annoyed, "I was *born* a woman. I'm becoming a man."

The room tilted. Everything got fuzzy around the edges. I remember we talked for a while, during which he explained a lot more than I ever expected to know about certain medical procedures and I explained that I was not "evolved" enough to continue dating him. My head was spinning for weeks.

In all likelihood, nothing this extreme will happen to you. You will probably, however, come across men who will surprise you by telling you they are gay or bisexual. You may also, at some time or other, be approached by a gay woman who is interested in you. When words fail you, due to your being in unfamiliar gender territory:

DATE LINES

"At least you had the balls to tell me." (This is admittedly a little mean; but maybe your transsexual won't be as nice as mine.)

"I knew this was too good to be true."

"Have you ever thought about switching to the other team?" (Reminder: This is a joke. In this ballpark the teams are pretty much set.)

"Well, do you know anybody just like you who is straight? A brother? A clone?"

"Wanna go man-hunting together?"

(To a gay woman) "Believe me, if that was my inclination at all, you'd be on my A list for sure, but alas, I am hopelessly hetero."

(To a bisexual man) "I'm afraid that's too advanced for me. I have enough trouble dealing with one sex."

The Ultimate Disaster: The Psycho Date

Strange date behavior can range from the unsettling to the dangerous. There are harmless, odd dates like the one my uncle once told me about: A beautiful woman cooked him a great dinner. Just as he was sitting back to enjoy his after-dinner cigar, thinking maybe she was *it*—The One—he heard her in the kitchen doing the dishes, and singing "The Star Spangled Banner" at the top of her lungs. (And it wasn't Independence Day. It wasn't even baseball season.)

And then there are the really *psycho* psycho dates like the Shrink Wrap Guy. The Shrink Wrap Guy was the result of a fix-up for my neighbor Doris by a friend of a friend of hers. He seemed quite normal at first, but by the second date some definite weirdness started surfacing: He confessed a penchant

---

HEAD FOR THE HILLS:
The Ten Bad Date Warning Signs

1. When the waiter asks if he wants a drink, your date says "No thanks, I brought my flask."

2. He shows up at your door with seven suitcases, and asks if he can leave them at your place "temporarily."

3. He tells you he's made reservations at a place called The Devil's Playhouse and that you will need a change of clothing.

4. The cosmetics mirror above the passenger seat in his car has "He's married, sweetheart!" scrawled on it in red lipstick.

5. It's your first date, and he tells you he's taking you to meet his parents— and their minister.

6. He's carrying a small whip, and you're *not* in horse country.

7. He takes his cell phone with him into the men's room.

8. He tells you his favorite movies feature someone named Candy Knockers.

9. On your walk to the movie theater, he stops and barks loudly at every dog he sees.

10. After you let him in, he looks nervously around and asks how much cash you have in the house.

---

for the international spy business; he made a few oblique but alarming allusions to an unusual religious upbringing. He also told Doris that his father had never once called him by his first name, not even as a baby. After this date, Doris sent him a polite we're-just-not-meant-to-be note. That's when she began to receive the shrink-wrapped packages.

They were all double shrink-wrapped (really *shrink-wrapped,* Doris told me, like packages you buy at the supermarket) and all had Xeroxed copies of her polite note affixed to the front. Behind those were long letters to Doris telling her what a mistake she had made. Several of these parcels came, then thankfully, they finally stopped. But Doris can never really look at shrink-wrapping the same again.

There are many forms of psycho dates, most of them too scary to talk about here. Always make sure you tell a friend the details of these encounters. And after you have sent the psycho packing, cut off all contact with him. Never argue with him; don't get into a debate about anything that happened on your date(s). Just get the heck out of there.

What *should* you say to your psycho date when he reveals his true nature?

 DATE LINES

"It's *absolutely* not you; it's *totally* me."

"When you're right, you're right!"

"Check, please!"

Chapter Ten:

DRY SPELLS: DEALING WITH DATELESSNESS

As far as I'm concerned, being any gender is a drag.
—PATTI SMITH

ometimes you can't even find a psycho to go out with. I can certainly recall countless times when, upon receiving an invitation, I'd say to myself, "Oh, god, how am I going to dig up a date for this thing?" And much of the time I didn't.

Luckily, I am now at the point in my life where I don't give a hoot (or is it a fig?) if I go places alone or not. In fact, unless I am in desperate need of a ride, I am sometimes happier going solo. That way, I arrive when I want, I leave when I want, and there is no one to tell me on the way home that I shouldn't have tangoed all night long with that mysterious, mustached stranger.

Nevertheless, I believe it is always a good idea—whether you've been stood up, you've recently broken up, or you just couldn't get a date—to have a pithy comeback ready for that well-intentioned (or maybe not so well-intentioned) meddler who inquires of you whether your nonexistent escort is hanging up your coat or parking the car.

Lines for the Unescorted

"It was so awful," my friend Gail moaned one day, remembering one particularly disastrous dateless situation. She had been invited to a black tie ball and really wanted to go (after all, she reasoned, how many times do you get the opportunity to waltz in the nineties?). After two weeks of trying to find someone willing to produce a tux *and* commit to dancing in it, she gave up and decided to go alone.

The day of the ball arrived. Upon entering the great hall she was greeted by her hostess, a perky blue-blood type from the South who had never in her life been without an escort and whose current husband owned a large chunk of Wall Street.

"Well Ha-ah, Gay-ale!" the hostess crooned, and then, "Goodness, where in the world's your date, honey-lamb?"

"Hi—um, no . . . well, I didn't bring one." Gail muttered, cheeks pink.

"You *didn't?* Well, why not, honey? I did say you could, didn't I? I mean, darlin', it *is* a day-ance, you know!"

According to Gail, the combination of acute embarrassment and annoyance at the hostess' insensitivity caused a bizarre glitch in what is otherwise a perfectly nice personality.

"DO YOU THINK I WOULD HAVE COME ALONE IF I COULD HAVE GOTTEN A DATE, YOU LITTLE

IDIOT?" she yelled, causing the swiveling of quite a few nearby heads. The hostess raised one perfectly plucked eyebrow, suggested Gail get a drink to "calm her poor little frazzled self," and left her standing there with egg on her by now bright red face.

How much better it might have been for Gail if she had thought to prepare a response to the hostess' irksome query in the form of one of the following lines.

DATE LINES

"Actually, I had a date with me but I lost him on the subway [freeway]."

"I decided not to bring a date; that way I can wolf other women's men."

"I came with a date, but right before we got here we had a fight, and he just took off somewhere." (Affect a gay Bette Davis smile here, along with a dramatic wave of the hand.)

"*Hey:* Did *Cinderella* have a date to the ball?"

"I'd have certainly brought a date, but considering the demand for single men, I didn't want to risk exposing mine to all these other hungry women!"

"A date? Oh, I couldn't get one—all the places I went to were sold out."

Being Stood Up: How Not to Take It Sitting Down

One of my least favorite memories is of the time I gave a party for the purpose of having my friends meet a guy I was dating. Said guy failed to appear, which was particularly embarrassing to me because the mutual friends who had originally set us up were at the party. But the worst part about this nightmarish evening was that everyone kept pulling me aside and whispering, "So where is he?" "Which one *is* he?" and I had to keep repeating, "He's not here," "I don't know where he is," and "He didn't show."

Let's hope you never have to suffer the pride-crippling ignominy of being stood up in any fashion. But if you do have to face people under these circumstances, it is often best to have a reply on hand, so you don't dissolve into tears while you are explaining ad nauseam how the schmuck never even called.

DATE LINES

(Whispering) "Oh, he's here. He's just very thin."

"Oh, *him?* I decided to give him the ax. And if he hadn't stood me up, he'd know it, too."

"Where's Joe? Joe *who?* I used to know someone named Joe. But he's been deleted from my memory."

"He must have had an emergency. And if he *didn't* have an emergency, he better make one up if I ever see him again, which is looking unlikely at this point."

"I believe I have been what is commonly referred to as 'stood up.' Isn't that a bizarre expression? What does it mean? Does it mean you are left standing alone in the rain? Does it mean you are going to have to stand up all night because you don't have an escort?"

"Joe had other plans I guess he forgot to tell me about. I think I'll forget to ever call him again."

After Breaking Up

People hate change. When they get used to seeing you with someone, they are disturbed when that someone isn't there anymore. Never mind that *you* are the one who just went through Hell breaking up with him; they always want to know when it happened, how it happened, and why.

One woman, Julie, described her difficulty coping with social events right after her breakup. She would be fine until someone would ask her where *he* was, and then she would dissolve into tears and make a dash for the bathroom. After a few episodes like this, she came up with the most creative way I have ever heard of to handle these moments.

Whenever she went to a party, she would attach a pair of flip-ups to her glasses, which she wore in the flipped up position. When someone would ask, "Where's Patrick?" she would snap them down. On the front of the flip-ups, now covering her eyes, was taped a typed message: "Patrick is gone for good. I don't want to talk about it. Thank you." The best thing about this innovation, Julie told me, was that she could keep the shades over her eyes until she was sure she was not going to cry, and until it was clear the person who had inquired was really going to desist.

I don't know whether this bizarre story is true or not, and I can understand that such a stunt would not be an option for most people. (Though I must confess it appeals to me.) For the less adventuresome, here are some other responses you might want to try when you've just broken up and you *don't* want to talk about it.

 ## DATE LINES

"Patrick? He was only my imaginary friend."

"Shhh. I killed him. Don't tell anyone."

"Patrick was like the measles. I caught him and went to bed with him for a while; now he's gone and I'm immune."

"Listen, they say change is important for spiritual and psychological growth. Let's just say I've been doing a lot of growing lately. Excuse me." (Exit with a smile.)

(Or try this simple subject changer.)
"I'm afraid we parted company. Speaking of company, is Marijo coming tonight? I hear she has a new job."

"Faux" Date Lines: When You Want People to Know It's Just a Platonic Thing

My mother always told me it didn't matter who you went to the party with, because you could always meet someone else once you got there. All I can say to this is Hrrummph. I don't know what things were like when my mother was young, but modern men—who are for the most part terrified of rejection—are easily discouraged if they think you might already be taken. The exceptions to this rule are 1) a man who is interested in adulterous liaisons, 2) a man who pursues women solely for the thrill of the conquest, or 3) a man who falls for you at first sight. In the first two cases, you are better off without him; in the last, it will either be true love or a total disaster, but in any case it won't matter too much *what* you say about who you happened to come to the party with that night.

My friend Toby once went to a wedding with an old friend (male). While in line for the buffet she found herself behind a gorgeous guy, and they began to chat. He was (apparently) single, *and* he was funny—her number one requirement in a man. Finally their plates were piled high and it was time to go back to the tables.

"Well," the man said kind of wistfully, "I guess your date is waiting for you back there."

"Oh, *him?*" Toby said much too quickly, and then, with an unintentional sharp edge to her voice, blurted out, *"He's not anybody."* The man looked at her oddly, murmured a hasty "Well anyway, see ya," and disappeared back into the crowd. Toby could tell he had decided he must have been wrong about her; only a totally uncouth person would say such a thing. And at that moment, she had to agree with him.

For those occasions when you don't want to go to the event alone but you *do* want people to know you are single, try these somewhat less abrasive lines.

DATE LINES

"Do you mean Bob? Oh, he is *so* great; he's like a brother to me."

"Have you met Bob? He was generous enough to act as my escort tonight."

"Do you happen to know if there are any nice gay men here I could introduce my friend Bob to?"

"*Bob* here is very knowledgeable about this subject. At least, his wife [girlfriend/boyfriend] is always telling me so!"

"Oh, yes, I did come with that man over there. (Pause) But that doesn't necessarily mean I am going home with him."

Anti-date Lines: When You Decide to Hang Up Your Dating Gloves for a While

What if—after dating five guys who went back to their wives, three who couldn't make a commitment, and two who just liked to borrow your clothes—you decide to throw in the towel and live a worry-free, dateless existence, at least temporarily? Believe me, you will need some comebacks to get you past your postdating demons—namely, your mother, your doorman, and your well-meaning friends who think that anyone who isn't married needs a therapist. Let them know how you feel about your solitary nonconfinement.

DATE LINES

"Dates are for fruit salad."

"I don't date anymore; I have affairs."

"After I read *Men Are from Mars, Women Are from Venus,* I decided to give up dating and become an astronaut."

"I ran out of dating fuel last year."

"I've seen what's out there and frankly, I'd rather stay home."

"I'd rather be single than married to Rush Limbaugh."

"I don't *do* relationships."

Chapter Eleven

SEX TALK

To err is human—but it feels divine.
—MAE WEST

f my mother is reading this, I have to tell her to please stop right here. (I mean it, Mom.) Okay, now that she's gone, we can get down to talking about talking about sex.

The whole topic is a pretty tricky one. (I was about to say sticky, but I knew I'd get groans.) Because often the idea of having sex is fraught with various levels of fear, guilt, confusion, animal passion, and mixed-up morality—not to mention health concerns—people have a greater unwillingness to express themselves about it, even though there is more need for humor in this area than almost any other. Of course there some super sacred or super steamy moments when no line is the best line, and speech would be superfluous. Still, the women I spoke with tended to agree that there are a lot of awkward moments when two people first decide to sleep together—moments when conversation is difficult and misunderstandings easy.

Between the Lines: Innuendos and Other Signal-Sending

Of course if your love life is like *Last Tango in Paris,* finding words to encourage him is not going to be an issue. But most people in real life will experience at least a little bit of fear or uncertainty as to whether or not the other person is on her wavelength. Innuendos, double entendres, and other sex signals are useful in letting the man know you're thinking in a positive way about becoming physically closer to him. Note: The following lines are for the most part pretty blatant, designed to inject humor—even silliness—into what might be an overly tense situation. If you want to be a bit more subtle (even subconscious), just work the following words into your conversation with the man (if he is alone with you in your apartment): *bed, bedroom, diaphragm, breasts, sex, intimacy, kiss, lips, tongue, foreplay, hips, longing, desire.* (Examples: "I had such a productive day—I got a new quilt for my bed." Or, "Watch it, don't step on my diaphragm case.")

DATE LINES

"They say the way to a man's heart is through his stomach, but how do I get to the other parts?"

"Is that a gun in your pocket or are you just carrying a really big comb?"

"Would you like to come up and see my etchings?"

"Do you have any interest in seeing my favorite freckle?"

"I love that tattoo. Got any more?"

"People say they live in fear of being tongue-tied; to me, it sounds kind of fun."

"Can I buy you a cup of aphrodisiac?"

"Will you go out with me . . . or even better, stay in with me?"

"How about coming up to my place for a bit of heavy breathing?"

For the Girl Who Can Say No

On the other hand, there are many times when you are going to want to put on the brakes. There are ways to say no without beating him over the head with a frying pan. (Of course, sometimes that pan may become necessary. As I have said before, some men don't understand "No" too well. Never feel guilty about this. Just keep saying it until he gets it.) But with most non-Neanderthals, you simply need a lighthearted way to tell him you are not ready to have sex with him. It can be a blow to his ego, but a little humor will help ease the intensity of the blow.

DATE LINES

"I'm definitely tempted; I'm also definitely not ready."

"Look, if I sleep with you I will fall madly in love with you and follow you around like Glenn Close, and I don't think either of us wants that."

"I may be easy on the eyes, but I'm hard to get."

"Being with you is heaven, but I'm no harp."

"You can come up for coffee but there's not going to be any sugar."

"Goodness, you have more arms than an octopus. Any more of that and I'll have to get out my harpoon."

"The only trouble with a man knowing a woman like a book is sometimes he forgets his place."

"Just because you picked me up doesn't mean I've fallen for you."

"Whoa—any further than that and we'll have to get blood tests!"

In Flagrante Dedicto: Some DOs and DON'Ts

One friend confessed to me that the first time she was intimate with her boyfriend, she found herself spouting baseball stats at crucial moments. She wasn't sure why; it just happened. She and her boyfriend never discussed it afterwards, but ever since then he has really loved taking her to ball games.

Here are some very general guidelines for coital conversation. (Mostly you should let nature take over.)

DATE LINES

DOs: "Hubba Hubba."

"You are one gorgeous hunk."

"When you do that, it drives me wild."

DON'Ts: "I'm usually in better shape than this."

"Honey, you really need to start going to the gym again."

"I can't wait for you to meet my parents."

"I can't wait to tell my therapist about this."

"Don't forget to pick up the tickets tomorrow, and I'll stop at the bank . . . what's the matter?"

What to say and what not to say about condoms

DO NOT SAY:

"Let's see: latex, polyurethane, or lambskin; ribbed, red, green, or rainbow?"

"This one's kind of old, but what the hey."

"Do you have any idea how to put this awful thing on?"

"I think this one looks too big for you."

"The last time I did this the condom broke."

DO SAY:

"Here, let me do that."

"Hmmm . . . I may need the jumbo size."

After the Fact: Postsex Lines

If all goes well, you are not going to need (or remember) any lines; all language barriers will have melted away. On the other hand, after sex you can feel as though you have just re-entered your brains after a long vacation, and getting them working again is like trying to start up an old car that's been sitting out in the cold. You have to learn how to talk again. And sometimes, one needs a little reassuring.

 ## DATE LINES

"Hello. Is the world still turning?"

"Wow. How did that happen?"

"Baby, you're the greatest!"

"Wow. I've heard that men are from Mars, but that was really out of this world!"

"This could be the beginning of a beautiful friendship."

"I think I'm a changed woman."

"That was the most fun I've had without laughing."

Chapter Twelve:

GOING EXCLUSIVE:
FURTHERING THE RELATIONSHIP

It was so cold I almost got married.
—SHELLY WINTERS

ongratulations. You found him, you dated him, and you've decided to keep him. Things are going along swimmingly, but you can still blow it if you can't find the right way to tell him where you would like the both of you to swim.

Lines for Suggesting Monogamous Dating or Living Together

With any luck, your "understanding" with your new man will develop naturally; however, once in a while the guy will need just a little push here and there. Be gentle with the pushing; men still have that fear-of-commitment thing. It's odd, but most men seem to go through their lives trying to avoid being "caught" by a woman; then after they are married, they generally love it. Whereas, most women go through their lives desperately looking for a man to marry, and after they are married they wonder why in the world they were so hell-bent on it in the first place.

Traditionally, one would ask one's main squeeze the important relationship questions over a romantic dinner. But traditionally, it was the man who asked the woman these kinds of questions. So why not forget tradition—and try these more innovative places for furthering your romance:

DATE LINES

(While looking up a phone number) "By the way, are you ready to rip up your little black book? I will if you will." (I know nobody actually has one of these anymore, but the image is still meaningful.)

(While clothes shopping) "I'm thinking we should change the fabric of our relationship. What do you think?"

(At the hardware store) "Here are your keys to my apartment. You already have the keys to my heart."

(At the bank) "Are you ready for joint accounting?"

(After getting your hair done) "I almost got a manicure too; I want to make sure if you are thinking of dating anyone else that I am equipped to scratch her eyes out."

(Or go retro, as you take his hand on the street) "Honey-bunch, let's go steady."

What to Say (or Not to Say) upon Meeting Friends/Family

I have listened to numerous accounts of people's introductions of their sweethearts to their families; most of these horror stories tend to center around mistakes made at the family dinner table. Usually the guest gets himself (or herself) into trouble through gross misuse of flattery—which he may think is his only hope of survival—or by saying something no parent wants to hear (like the fact that he doesn't believe in working). One man I know joked about how he was "still single" at his longtime girlfriend's family Thanksgiving dinner. (He had no idea why all the women at the table were appalled; none of the other men noticed, either.) Sometimes there is an inadvertent insult to the mother's (or father's) cooking, or careless talk about a jointly owned cat when the family doesn't even know the couple is living together.

Meeting your loved one's family can be traumatic, but it is nothing compared to the ordeal meeting his friends can be. The best story I ever heard about this came from a lovely woman I met on a plane. On or about her fourth date with her current boyfriend, he invited her to meet him at a particular restaurant. When she arrived, the restaurant appeared to be closed, but a surly manager type grunted at her, "He's in the back." Somewhat apprehensively, she went through the door the man indicated.

There, sitting around a large round table, were seven or eight men—one of whom was, thankfully, her boyfriend. They smiled at her and pointed to the one empty chair at the table.

"Please have a seat," said one guy. "Sorry to do this to you, but our good friend here"—he nodded at her boyfriend—"has made so many disastrous mistakes in his love life that we decided we were going to interview any of his serious prospects." And interview her they did—for two hours. (She said it was more like an inquisition.) Happily, she passed the test; and last I heard she was still together with her boyfriend, who I gathered was well worth being ambushed for.

 ## DATE LINES

To His Mother:

What to Say: "You have a lovely home."

What Not to Say: "Yes, I would love to have a second helping of this delicious green marshmallow-Jell-O fruit mold." (This kind of sacrificial flattery is a major mistake. You'll be eating the stuff for the rest of your life.)

To His Father:

What to Say: "You look too young to be Joe's father."

What Not to Say: "You are an *audaciously* handsome devil."

To His Child (If he has one):

What to Say: "Your father talks about you, and how wonderful you are, all the time."

What Not to Say: "You want me to be your mommy?"

To His Friends:

What to Say: "So what do you guys want to watch?"

What Not to Say: "Please don't encourage my Andy to drink so much beer."

The World's Best Marriage Proposals

It is nowadays quite acceptable, thank goodness, for the woman to do the question-popping. But before you come right out and ask him, "Hey, do ya wanna just get married?" while you're sitting around watching *Nightline,* give some serious thought to how you want this moment to be remembered. It's not as important for you as it is for your possible offspring, who will all want to know how Mommy asked Daddy to marry her. It's really fun later on to have a good proposal story. In fact, I sometimes think the proposing part is more important than the wedding. After all, when are you *really* making your commitment to each other?

Many people feel that as long as they are going to propose, they might as well do it big. By big, I mean in skywriting at halftime at the Super Bowl, on an airplane banner at the beach, or sending a nude singing telegram. What you should *never* do, in my opinion, is be one of these people who gets engaged on a TV talk show. If you are going to stray from the traditional down-on-one-knee "Will you marry me?" (which, by the way, is especially nice when done by the woman to the man), please do not stray by going on television. (I think your marriage is automatically doomed if you do this—though your offspring will at least get to watch the video.)

One of the cleverest, silliest proposals I heard of was from a man (Fred) to a woman (Jane). The couple sat down one Friday night to watch a video; but unbeknownst to Jane, Fred had prearranged for the video store to slip his own tape into the box instead of the movie they had "chosen." When the video began to play, there was a wide shot of some trees, then slowly the camera zoomed in on one tree. In the tree was Fred, jumping up and down, scratching himself and making monkey noises. The camera closed in on Fred's face and he said, "Let's stop monkeying around. Let's get married, Jane."

Obviously, most of the "mate lines" below are meant to be the precursor to "Will you marry me?" which, as cliched as they are, are usually the words that must be said, although you don't have to be legally married in order to mate for life.

MATE LINES

"Everyone else I ever dated was the first course; you are the entree."

"You are like a tune I've been trying to remember all my life."

"It's as if all my life I was listening to the warm-up band, until I met you."

"Let's face it, sweetheart, we're not getting any older!"

"Men are like corks: some pop the question, but most of them have to be drawn out."

Or, from *A Streetcar Named Desire:* "You need somebody and I need somebody, can't it be you and me, Blanche?" (Do make *sure* you call him "Blanche").

"Honey, let's get hitched [marry/get legal/do that holy wedlock thing/get state sanctioned.]"

"Sweetie, we really need something for this wall. How about a marriage license?"

If you are in a position to use any of the lines in this chapter, congratulations! You've successfully escaped the torments of the Dating Pond and have entered into the torments of a Relationship. Hopefully he's a keeper.

On the other hand, if your search for the Holy Male continues, don't lose hope. No matter what anybody says, there are plenty of frogs in the Pond, and with the help of a fun date line or two you might just catch one you like—warts and all.

Index